Becoming
A KNIGHT
FOR JESUS CHRIST

Becoming a Knight for Jesus Christ

Trilogy Christian Publishers

A Wholly Owned Subsidary of Trinity Broadcasting Network

2442 Michelle Drive

Tustin, CA 92780

Scripture quotations marked kjv are taken from the King James Version of the Bible. Public domain.

For information, address Trilogy Christian Publishing

Rights Department, 2442 Michelle Drive, Tustin, Ca 92780.

Trilogy Christian Publishing/ TBN and colophon are trademarks of Trinity Broadcasting Network.

For information about special discounts for bulk purchases, please contact Trilogy Christian Publishing.

Manufactured in the United States of America

10 9 8 7 6 5 4 3 2 1

Library of Congress Cataloging-in-Publication Data is available.

ISBN: 978-1-68556-062-1

ISBN: 978-1-68556-063-8

FORWARD

This study is for the purpose of becoming more like Jesus. These are outlines from different classes that I have taught over the years that I have put into order. I hope that these will help each person grow in their relationship with Jesus Christ. The most important thing in the world is not our health, or how much we have. The most important thing is that we have a relationship with Jesus Christ. I mean to have an intimate, personal relationship. This study will help you to grow and develop an intimate relationship.

In the back, are three supplemental materials. First of all, is a Bible reading schedule. This is reading the New Testament. It should be done during the first half of this course. Secondly, is a Surrender List. This should be filled out after section five, Seeker of the Hero. Once this is filled out, each item on the list is to be prayerfully given to Jesus and then the list should be burned. This is represented of the sacrifice that could not be taken back, and once these are surrendered to Jesus Christ, we should not take them back. The last item is a certificate. This is to be signed by the person giving the material.

This study is best done on a one-to-one basis or maybe a few people at a time with one person acting as a mentor/ teacher. If you are doing it on your own, ask the Holy Spirit to be your teacher and guide. I also recommend that as you are going through this study that you limit the amount of outside information coming into your brain. This way one can listen more to the direction and teaching of the Holy Spirit. All scripture in this guide is from the King James Version of the Holy Bible.

My hope is that you will enjoy these lessons as much as I enjoyed making them and teaching them. Ecclesiastes 4:12 says, "a threefold cord is not quickly broken." We have a threefold guide: we have a perfect teacher which is the Holy Spirit, our salvation is complete in a perfect Savior, Jesus Christ, and we have the perfect Word of God, the Bible. With these three we cannot lose.

Enjoy and may Jesus Christ bless you.

Jeff Kissell

TABLE OF CONTENTS

Forward 3

Introduction 7

Seeker of Wisdom 13

Seeker of Truth 33

Seeker of Comfort 63

Seeker of Guidance 71

Seeker of a Hero 89

Seeker of Servanthood 159

Seeker of Change 177

Supplemental Material 203

INTRODUCTION

As with any program, there must be a purpose. The purpose of this study is to become a disciple of Jesus. This is accomplished through prayer, Bible study and working through the different levels of being a Seeker. Before one can come to the truth, one must seek to know the truth.

The levels of Seeking are:

1. Seeker of Wisdom—this is seeking to know more about God.

2. Seeker of Truth—this is seeking to know more about Jesus.

3. Seeker of Comfort—this is seeking to know more about the Holy Spirit.

4. Seeker of Guidance—this is seeking to know more about the Bible.

5. Seeker of a Hero—this is seeking to know more about those who have been faithful.

6. Seeker of Servanthood—this is seeking to know more about where we have our place.

7. Seeker of Change—this is seeking to become more like our Lord and Savior, Jesus Christ.

Once the seventh level is complete then one becomes a Knight of the Cross. This allows for the Knight to teach and train up others to also become Knights of the Cross.

The symbol is the cross and the crown. This is a reference

to Jesus enduring the cross in order to obtain the crown. We also must be willing to endure the cross that we are to bear so that at the end of the training we can also wear the crown. As it is with this study, so it is with life. As we strive to become more like Jesus, we will overcome the temptations and let go of the weights that would hinder our growth. The goal is to become more like Jesus and less like ourselves. We put the old man (ourselves) on the cross and take up the new man (who we are in Christ) daily. This allows us to take on the image of Christ.

The journey may be long and bumpy, but the end is worth it. Are you ready to begin?

THE FALL AND SALVATION OF MAN

A. Man was created in the image and likeness of God Genesis 1:26-27, Genesis 2:7 Psalms 8:4-8

    a. Man is created good

    b. Man is created upright

    c. Man is created with intelligence

        i. Reason

        ii. Solve problems

        iii. To think

    d. Man is created with a conscience

        i. Ability to chose

        ii. God placed his law in us and we can choose to obey

    e. Man is created with a will

        i. To obey or not

    f. Man is created with a soul

        i. To live eternally

    g. Man is created for fellowship with God

B. Man fell when he rejected God's plan, and sin entered the picture Genesis 3:1-6

    h. Sin is a word that means "to miss the mark"

    i. Sin causes us to miss our purpose in life, fellowship

with God

j.   Sin is disobedience to God's authority

   i.   We choose what seems right rather than what is right

   ii.   Results of sin—

      1.   Sorrow

      2.   Sickness

      3.   Pain

      4.   Death

      5.   Separation from God

   iii.   How do we react without God?

      1.   Romans 1:18-32

      2.   Isaiah 5:20-23

      3.   Romans 3:9-18

C.   Man tries to reestablish this relationship on his own, and comes far short, thus becoming "religious"—God hates religion.

D.   ONLY GOD CAN REESTABLISH THIS RELATIONSHIP

   a.   Salvation is from God, not man Romans 6:23

   i.   It was thought by God the Father, bought by the Son, and wrought by the Spirit, and man has no part in planning or purchasing it

   ii.   Salvation is through Christ alone   Acts 4:12, Luke 19:10, Matthew 10:28, Ephesians 1:7, Hebrews 9:22

   iii.   Salvation is by grace and not works Ephesians 2:8-10

   iv.   A sacrifice had to be made Genesis 22:8,

      1.   A substitute could be found—animal sacrifices Lev. 17:14

2. Jesus was the ultimate sacrifice

   a. He had to be pure and holy, without sin

   b. He had to be God in order to take man's place

v. Salvation is completed with Jesus's blood

   b. Justification is obtained when we accept God's gift

   c. Man has to be willing to accept this gift of salvation

i. God has done the work, man must respond

   1. Repentance—a sincere and complete change of mind in regard to sin

     a. Intellectual element—a change of view—seeing oneself as God sees him

     b. Emotional element—feeling of deep sorrow and guilt—Holy Spirit convicts us of our sin

     c. Volitional element—we are given the right and ability to make the decision—man is now responsible for his own salvation by his choice

   2. Faith—the ability to receive what we do not have   John 1:12

   3. Obedience—we will obey what God tells us to do.

     a. We become new creatures in Christ—2 Corinthians 5:17 Ephesians 4:21-24

     b. We become righteous Philippians 3:9

    c.   There will be outward evidence, and inward evidence—

        i.   Joy of salvation

        ii.   The Holy Spirit bears witness with our spirit—Romans 8:15-16

        iii.   Love for others 1 John 4:7

        iv.   Impartation of the Holy Spirit 1 John 4:13

        v.   Ephesians 4:22-32

E.   The choice is up to us!!

LEVEL 1

Seeker of Wisdom

For the Lord giveth wisdom:
out of his mouth cometh knowledge and understanding.
Proverbs 2:6

If any of you lack wisdom, let him ask of God
James 1:5

ONE TRUE GOD

A. What are some of the concepts of God today?

    a. The "man upstairs"

    b. The big "candy man in the sky"

    c. An impersonal being who doesn't care

    d. He doesn't exist. Psalms 14:1

    e. God is in all of us, so we are gods—new age

    f. One to be avoided at all costs

    g. The "universal mind"

B. We believe that there is ONE TRUE GOD

    h. What God is not—

        i. Not polytheistic—having belief in many gods

        ii. Not materialistic—that the universe constitutes all the god there is

        iii. Not pantheistic—the belief that God is all, and all is God

        iv. Not deistic—a God who is removed from His creation

    i. What God is—

        i. God is eternal—not limited by time Isaiah 43:10

        ii. God is self-existent—has always been

        iii. God is the Creator of all—Genesis 1:1

        iv. God is non-created—no one created God

    v.   God is omnipresent –God is not limited by space Psalms 139:7-12

    vi.   God is omnipotent—no limit to His power

    vii.   God is omniscient—God is all knowing Psalms 147:5

    viii.   God is a Spirit-Person—our conviction of God is faith based John 4:24

    ix.   God knows the future—prophecy is no problem for God

    x.   God is unchanging—He doesn't change Malachi 3:6,

    xi.   God is perfect

    xii.   God is holy

    xiii.   God is just

    xiv.   God is good

    xv.   God is love

    xvi.   God is truth

    xvii.   God redeems/saves/rescues man from sin—Isaiah 43:11

j.   God has revealed Himself as a single being consisting of three interrelated persons: the Father, the Son, and the Holy Spirit

    i.   Zechariah 14:9, Genesis 1:2, Genesis 1:26-27, Joel 2:28

    ii.   Each is distinct in office from the others

    iii.   The three cooperate with one mind and purpose

    iv.   They are perfectly one in character

and harmony, and so constitute one "God-head"

v. They are one in essence and activity Matt 28:19, Luke 3:22

k. We may know God as Father, just like Jesus did. John 5:16-47

    i. The Jews did not have this type of relationship with God—They considered Abraham their father, not God

    ii. Why did the Jews try to kill Jesus? —He broke the Sabbath, and He made Himself equal to God

    iii. How does this passage support the doctrine of the Trinity? –The Father and the Son are separate and distinct, yet they work in unity to accomplish their will

l. We may know Jesus as the Son, and as Savior

    i. The Jews were looking for a deliverer, but not as a "suffering servant." Thus, they rejected Jesus.

    ii. Jesus did the work for us to have a relationship with the Godhead. If Jesus had been an ordinary man, He could not have fulfilled the sacrifice needed.

m. We may know the Power and Direction that come from the Holy Spirit

    i. Jesus said that we would receive Power

        ii. Just as Jesus was led by the Spirit, so can we be led today

    n. Jesus commanded the use of the Trinity

        i. Matthew 28:18-19

        ii. Jesus is given all authority, which only God has. Jesus in John 5:22-27 is the judge, again a position reserved for God. Jesus told us that the Holy Spirit would be an advocate or comforter after He returns to the Father. (John 14:16)

        iii. The Holy Spirit will not speak of Himself, but what comes from the Father and Jesus (John 15:26)

        iv. All three were present at the baptism of Jesus in Mark 1:9-13

            1. What role do the Father, Son, and Holy Spirit play in this passage? —The Son is baptized, the Holy Spirit descends, and the Father announced His approval

    o. Nowhere in the New Testament is the doctrine of Trinity explained. It is assumed that the readers will understand and be familiar with the teaching, unlike the doctrine of salvation or the Church.

C. This doctrine is difficult to understand, because with our minds, we cannot understand this, and there are not any real examples of this in nature.

JESUS CHRIST IS FULLY GOD AND FULLY MAN

A. Jesus is God

    a. God will provide Himself a ram—Genesis 22:8

    b. He had always existed - Revelation 1:8 John 1:1

    c. He created all things—Colossians 1:16-17

    d. His virgin birth declares Him as God—Luke 1:31-35

    e. His sinless life declares He is God—1 Peter2: 22 Hebrews 4:15

    f. He worked miracles that only God could do—Acts 2:22, 10:38

        i. Miracles of people—huge numbers of them

            1. Leprosy

            2. Paralysis

            3. Blindness

            4. Fever

            5. Death

        ii. Miracles of nature—a lot of those as well

            1. Water into wine

            2. Calming the storm

      3. Fig tree withering

      4. Fish with coin in its mouth

      5. Fed multitude with few fish & bread

      6. Walked on water

  g. He forgave sin, and only God can do that—Mark 2:9-11

  h. He died on a cross and paid the debt for all mankind with His blood—1 Corinthians 15:3

  i. He rose from the dead three days, just like He said—Matthew 28:6 1 Corinthians 15:14

  j. He ascended into Heaven and is seated at the right hand of God—Hebrews 1:3

  k. He is waiting for the time to claim His inheritance, the Church

B. Jesus was completely man

  l. Jesus got tired—slept in the boat

  m. Jesus got hungry—He asked for bread

  n. Jesus mourned for Lazarus

  o. Jesus was thirsty on the cross

  p. Jesus felt the pain of the crucifixion

  q. Jesus exhibited all human emotions, only to the fullest

  r. Jesus was tempted, but did not yield

  s. Jesus died and was buried

GOD

Is God a whom or a what?

Definition: "God is a spirit, infinite, eternal and unchangeable in His being, wisdom, power, holiness, justice, goodness and truth"—Westminster Catechism

The Bible does not give an explanation of God, it is a given that He exists. God has revealed Himself by His name, which tell not only who He is, but also reveals what He is.

A. Names of God—name expresses His whole being

    a. ELOHIM— "God"—this is the creative Power and omnipotence of God—Creator (it is plural which signifies the trinity and the fullness of the godhead) Genesis 1:1

    b. JEHOVAH— "LORD"—revealing Himself to man—(Exodus 3:13-14) God does not stand far from his creation, but is available to help them. In Exodus 3:14, God tells Moses he is "I AM THAT I AM." We get the name from the letters of YHWH. Hebrew has no vowels, so they inserted the vowels from another name for God, ADONAI, and got "YAHWEH," or JEHOVAH. Exodus 6:2-3   Psalms 83:18 What God does for His people is expressed in His names

        i. JEHOVAH-RAPHA—THE LORD THAT HEALS Exodus 15:26

        ii. JEHOVAH-NISSI—THE LORD OUR BANNER Exodus 17:15

        iii. JEHOVAH-SHALOM—THE LORD OUR PEACE Judges 6:24

        iv. JEHOVAH-RA'AH—THE LORD MY SHEP-

HERD Psalms 23:1

 v. JEHOVAH-TSIDKENU—THE LORD OUR RIGHTEOUSNESS Jeremiah 23:6

 vi. JEHOVAH-JIREH—THE LORD WHO PRO-VIDES Genesis22: 14

 vii. JEHOVAH-SHAMMAH—THE LORD IS THERE Ezekiel 48:35

 viii. JEHOVAH-MEKADDISHKEM—THE LORD OUR SANCTIFIER Exodus 31:13

 ix. JEHOVAH-SABAOTH—THE LORD OF HOSTS Isaiah 37:16, I Samuel 1:3-11, Joshua 5:13-15

 x. JEHOVAH-HOSEENU—THE LORD OUR MAKER Psalms 95:6

c. EL— "God" this is used in combinations

 i. EL-ELYON—THE MOST HIGH GOD Genesis 14:18-20

 ii. EL-SHADDAI—THE GOD WHO MEETS THE NEEDS OF HIS PEOPLE Exodus 6:3

 iii. EL-OLAM—THE EVERLASTING GOD Genesis 21:33

d. ADONAI—LORD—This is Lord or Master, Sovereign, and has the concept of dominion and rule. Thomas calls Jesus this when he declares "My Lord and my God."

 i. ADONAI-JEHOVAH—THE LORD OUR SOVEREIGN—Master Jehovah Genesis 15:2

e. FATHER—describes God as the creator of all. However, it deals with a special relationship. That is what WE have with God if we have accepted Jesus as our

Lord and Savior. The Lord's Prayer shows this.

B. God's name is how he reveals HIMSELF to his people. It is with the name that we worship, by calling upon His name. We are to praise the name of God. His name is to be feared. We glorify the name of God. We are to hallow His name. God defends his people because of His name, and He will not forsake them. WE ARE NOT TO TAKE THE NAME OF THE LORD IN VAIN, NOR TO PROFANE OR BLAS-PHEME GOD'S NAME.

C. Attributes of God—God's attributes show sides of His character.

    f.   God is a Spirit—John 4:24

        i.   He thinks, feels, speaks, and communicates.

        ii. Not limited by body

        iii. God can manifest Himself in a way that we can understand. Genesis 18:1

    g. God is infinite—not subject to natural and human limitations

        i.   He is not limited by space, but is characterized by immensity—I Kings 8:27

        ii. God is not limited by time, but is eternal Psalms 90:2

    h. God is ONE—Exodus 20:3, Deuteronomy 6:4

        i.   A compound unity—the three are in one

    i.   God is Omnipotent—all powerful Genesis 1:1

    j.   God is Omnipresent—everywhere, unlimited by space

    k. God is Omniscient—all knowing Psalms 94:9- God foresees but does not fix.

    l.   God is wise—He is able to direct our lives

    m. God is Sovereign—He has absolute right to govern as HE pleases Daniel 4:35

n.   God is Holy—He is morally pure. He cannot sin nor tolerate sin. He is separated from US in character and in nature Isaiah 6:3

o.   God is Righteous—God is righteous in His dealings with US Genesis 18:25 He also requires righteousness Romans 4:5.

p.   God is Faithful—He is absolutely trustworthy, and His promises will never fail

q.   God is Merciful—God has made provision for US, His creation to come to Him. He is patient and long-suffering toward us. This leads us to Hope in Jesus Christ, the ultimate act of MERCY to US.

r.   God is Love—It is because of this that God wants to have a personal relationship with US. God's love is manifested to us in Jesus Christ John 3:16

s.   God is Good—It is because of God's Goodness that He gives the blessings to US Psalms 25:8

t.   God is Jealous—God will not share His Glory with another Exodus 34:14, Deuteronomy 5:9

D. GOD IS DESERVING OF OUR PRAISE.

u.   "How big is God? How great and wide his vast domain. To try to tell, these lips can hardly start. He's big enough to rule this mighty universe, yet small enough to live with in my heart.

v.   We need to pursue the knowledge of God.

HEARING FROM GOD

A. Receiving God's Best by:

   a. Wanting God's Best

   b. Making Jesus our Focus

   c. Being in a relationship with Jesus

   d. Meditating on the Bible

   e. Make friends with the Holy Spirit

   f. *HEARING GOD'S WORD*

B. How does God speak to us?

   g. Through His Word

   h. Through pastors and counselors

   i. Dreams and visions

   j. Circumstances

   k. Holy Spirit

   l. Creation

C. What is to be our response?

   m. We must first *HEAR* the voice of God

   i. This comes through practice—we do not hear what God is saying with our natural ability or senses.

   ii. We must be *tuned in* to recognize Him— (Exodus15: 26, John 10:27)

   1. Must not only hear it but will know (this would mean having *KNOWLEDGE about* God. 2 Peter 1:3)

   2. We must belong to the Shepherd

25

    iii. We need to read/study Scripture

    iv. Must compare with Scripture—Acts 17:11-12

    v. Some of the ways we hear from God Satan will imitate and make us question. That is why we must compare it to what God has said in the Bible. God will never contradict what He has said. He never changes.

    vi. *IT IS NOT ENOUGH TO JUST HEAR THE VOICE OF GOD; WE MUST ALSO ACT ON WHAT WE HEAR.*

n. We must then *OBEY* the voice of God

    i. Key to all of God's blessings—Deuteronomy 28:1-2, v.15—if we fail to obey

    ii. Our health is dependent on obedience—Exodus 15:26

    iii. Our relationship with God is dependent on obedience—Jeremiah 7:23

        1. God wants our obedience rather than our sacrifice—Jeremiah 7:22, 1 Samuel 15:22

        2. THE SUCCESS OF OUR RELATIONSHIP WITH GOD AND OUR WALK WITH HIM DEPENDS ON HEARING HIS VOICE.

    iv. Our relationship with Jesus is the same—John 10:27

    v. In our relationship, we need to be swift to obey what God is asking us to do—Example—Abraham and Noah

    vi. Sometimes what God is asking us to do will seem foolish to other people. Often other Christians may even try to turn us from doing what God wants with clever arguments.

    vii.   We must be careful what we listen to/and think about—Philippians 4:8

    viii.   We must be careful who we listen to—2 Timothy 2:16-18, Ephesians 5:11-12

o.   We must take the time to *LISTEN* to God—this can go along with meditating on the Word, but we also need to have the discipline to "be still and KNOW THAT I AM GOD"—Psalms 46:10

OUR RESPONSE TO GOD

What does God want from us?

Deuteronomy 10:12-14, I Kings 8:56-61,
Micah 6:6-8, James 1:26-27

A. In the garden, God had fellowship with Adam and Eve. Since God does not change, it stands to reason that He also desires fellowship with us.

   a. *Fellowship with God*—I John 1:3-4 *Result of fellowship with God—That our joy may be full!*

   b. *Fellowship with one another*—I John 1:6-7, Acts 2:42 This will also be a result of fellowship with God, that we will want to have fellowship with each other.

   c. *Fellowship in the Gospel*—Philippians 1:4-6 We will enjoy spreading the Good News with others.

   d. *Fellowship in the sufferings of Christ*—Philippians 3:10 Jesus said we are to rejoice when we are to suffer persecution for His namesake.

   e. *No fellowship with darkness*—Ephesians 5:11, II Corinthians 6:14-18

B. In the garden, God was worshiped for who He is. We are to also worship God for who He is, as well as for the many blessings He has given to US.

   f. After the fall, one of the first acts we find is worship with an offering. (Cain and Able). Later we find Noah worshiping, again with an offering. Abraham and Isaac went to worship, again with an offering (Genesis 22:5) Through most of the Old Testament, the act of worship is tied to sacrifice, but it is much more. In the Law, there were specific ways of worship with sacrifice.

    i.   WORSHIP—to ascribe worth to something, acclaim it to a special position, *the reverent love and allegiance accorded a deity*, honor.

    ii. God is very specific about His idea of worship to another. HE WILL NOT TOLERATE IT. He is a Jealous God.

    iii. The people of Israel were driven from their land because of worshiping other gods.

g. Many different ways to worship—we worship with sacrifice, with tithes and offerings, with our music, with our prayers, with our time, with our lives. Everything we do should be an act of WORSHIP to GOD.

h. David set singers and others in the Temple to Worship God.

i. The Psalms are full of exhortations to *praise and worship* God.

    i.   Psalms 22:22-29, 29:1-11, 66:1-20, 95:1-11, 100:1-5

    ii. In New Testament—Jesus accepted worship John 20:28

C. In the garden, what was lacking was OBEDIENCE. This is one thing that God wants from us. He requires it, and it was because of this that Adam and Eve were forced from His presence; they had lost their covering of righteousness and were therefore naked.

    j. Again, OBEDIENCE is required throughout Genesis, with Able, Noah, and Abraham. Exodus 19:1-6—People are told to obey God and keep His commands. Exodus 23:20-25—The Angel spoken of here is none other than Jesus, the second person of the trinity. They were told to obey Him, and there will be blessing.

k.   Asked the question—Are there strings attached to the blessings of God and to being fruitful? The answer is *YES* Deuteronomy 11:26-32, Deuteronomy 28-30 (28:1-2, 15, 29:9, 30:1-3)

l.   God wants *OBEDIENCE rather than sacrifice*—I Samuel 15:9-23 (note verse *22-23*)

m.   If you want God's best for your life, then we must obey and serve Him—*Job 36:11-12*

n.   What about the New Testament? Aren't we under GRACE, and not the LAW? This is true, yet Jesus said that if we loved Him, we would keep His command-ments—*John 14:15*. This is where the Grace comes in. God is being so patient with US that He is forgiving us when we do not obey. I think it breaks His heart that we take His Word so lightly and not seriously. He has not changed.

o.   What if we do not obey—then what will happen? Jere-miah 12:17, 18:10, Revelation 3:15-16

D.   One last item that God wants from us is to FEAR Him. This is not to be in terror of Him, but rather to have a reverence and respect of Him and the things that are His.

p.   People are told to FEAR the Lord, and this is tied in with obedience. I Samuel 12:12-25

q.   Psalms are full of verses to FEAR the Lord—Psalms 2 (v11) 19:1-14, 22, 25:1-22, 33:1-22, 34:1-22.

r.   Proverbs 1:7—the beginning of knowledge. I Peter 1:3-4

s.   How do we perfect Holiness in our lives—in the FEAR OF GOD—II Corinthians 7:1

t.   We need to have that respect and sense of awe about God. It is easy for the things of God to become com-monplace and routine. Then we begin to grow cold, like the Church of Laodicea.

E. God has done the first part. He paid the price for us to come to Him. We now must work at keeping ourselves clean, and spotless and white so that when He returns, WE will be ready, like a bride on her wedding day, spotless and Holy. Psalms 51, I Peter 1:14-17

F. God wants that same relationship as in Eden. We need to work at keeping OUR end of the relationship.

LEVEL 2

Seeker of Truth

And the Word was made flesh, and dwelt among us,
(and we beheld his glory, the glory as of the only
Begotten of the Father,) full of grace and truth.
John 1:14

Jesus saith unto him, I am the way, the truth, and the life
John 14:6

HISTORY OF JESUS

A. Jesus Pre-existence➔HE IS GOD

B. Jesus's birth➔Immanuel—GOD WITH US

    a. Virgin Birth

    b. Bethlehem

    c. Flight to Egypt

    d. Return to Nazareth

C. Jesus early life

    e. Taught in Synagogue

    f. Taught a trade➔Carpenter

    g. Jerusalem for Bar-mitzvah— (at 12 years old)

D. Jesus Ministry

    h. Nazareth

    i. Galilee

    j. Jerusalem

E. Jesus Miracles

    k. Water to Wine

    l. Healing sick

    m. Raising dead

    n. Feeding multitudes

    o. Control over nature

    p. Control over demons

F. Jesus Passion— (Last week)

    q. Triumphal Entry to Jerusalem

    r.   Teaching

    s.   Last Supper

    t.   Arrest

    u.   Trial

    v.   Crucifixion

    w. Death

    x.   Resurrection➜Defeating Death

G. Jesus Ascension

H. Jesus Return and Reign

THE LIFE OF CHRIST

A. Before Bethlehem—Jesus was in Heaven, at one with the Father and the Holy Spirit

    a. Jesus is GOD—John 1:1-4, 10-14

        i. In the beginning was the WORD—And the WORD was GOD

        ii. All things were made by HIM—only GOD can CREATE

        iii. Hebrews 1:2—HE made the worlds

        iv. In HIM was LIFE—only GOD can give LIFE

        v. V.10—the world was made by HIM—only GOD can CREATE

        vi. V.12—gave HE power to become the sons of GOD—only GOD can do this

        vii. V.14—*the WORD became FLESH and dwelt among US!*

    b. Jesus is ETERNAL—Revelation 1:8, Colossians 1:16-17, Genesis 1:1

        i. Revelation 1:8—the beginning and the end, which is, and which was, and which is to come

        ii. Colossians 1:16-17—HE is before all things

        iii. By HIM were all things created

        iv. V, 17—By HIM all things consist—All things are maintained (Kept running) by HIM

        v. Genesis 1:1—In the beginning GOD created…

    c. Jesus is equal to GOD—Philippians 2:6-8

    i.   V. 6—being in the form of GOD➔equal with GOD

    ii.   John 5:17-18—Jesus says "My Father works, and I work"—V. 18-makes HIMSELF equal to GOD

    iii.   John 8:58—I AM➔the name God gave to Moses to reveal Himself—Jesus continues to use it. IE. I AM the Bread of Life, I AM the way, I AM the Light of the World, …

    iv.   *John 5:23➔SON and FATHER will have EQUAL HONOR*

  d.   Jesus did things that only GOD can do

    i.   Forgive sins—Mark 2:7-10

    ii.   Raises the dead—John 5:21, 11:38-44

    iii.   Will be the JUDGE of all men—John 5:22, and 27, I Peter 4:5

    iv.   Control over creation—walk on water, calm storms, multiply food, catch fish, etc.

B. At Bethlehem

  e.   Galatians 4:4—Fullness of time—MADE OF A WOMAN, made under the law

  f.   Philippians 2:7—Form of a SERVANT, and was made in the likeness of MEN

  g.   V. 8—HUMBLED HIMSELF and became_*Obedient*

    i.   Obedient to His humanity

       1.   BABY IN A MANGER

       2.   NEED FOR FOOD/DRINK

       3.   NEED TO REST

       4.   FELT PITY, SORROW, ANGER *(yet without sin—Hebrews 4:15)*

      ii.   Obedient to His "Parents"—Luke 2:51

      iii. Obedient to the Law➔goes to Jerusalem, Passover, Temple tax, etc.

h.   Jesus was born in Bethlehem to fulfill Prophecy—Micah 5:2 (Luke 2:4, Matthew 2:1)

i.   Born is stable—most likely a cave, and laid him in a manger➔this was used as a sign to the shepherds

j.   Circumcised the 8th day, ACCORDING TO THE LAW

k.   Given the name "JESUS"—Greek form of Joshua, which means "the LORD saves"—Matthew 1:21

l.   When Jesus is about two years old, (could be anywhere from 41 days to two years) {Leviticus 12:2-4} the Wise Men come

      i.   1st to Herod in Jerusalem, then to Bethlehem (about 5 miles)

      ii.   They enter the HOUSE

      iii. They saw the CHILD

      iv. They WORSHIPED JESUS

m. The family flees to EGYPT to escape Herod's attempt to kill Him. (Hosea 11:1) How long they are there, we are not sure. Herod died in 4 B.C.

n.   The family returns to Israel—Matthew 2:19-20

o.   The family sets up housekeeping in Galilee, in the town of Nazareth➔where they had been living before going to Bethlehem—Luke 2:4, Luke 1:26-27 (Unsure about the prophecy—a few believe that the word for "branch" in Hebrew is "NESER", which is where the name for Nazareth comes from. Also, Nazareth had a bad reputation (John 1:46), and some feel that Isaiah 11:1, Psalms 22:6, and Isaiah 53:3 go to make this work. However, others say it is a "spoken" prophecy and not a written down one. I don't think so because

Matthew is so careful to get the others right.

p.   At age of 12 Jesus has His BAR-MITZVAH—He is now considered a "son of the law" by most Jewish standards—Could now participate in the Synagogue Worship

q.   Jesus stays in Jerusalem, and is later found with the "doctors of the law," hearing them and asking them questions

r.   They were "astonished" at His understanding and questions (Isaiah 50:4 The Holy Spirit is teaching and bringing things to him remembrance {Mind like Adam} Psalms 119:97-104)

s.   Jesus returned with them to Nazareth and was "subject" unto them. Luke 2:51

t.   Jesus then grew in four ways—Luke 2:52

     i. In WISDOM

    ii. In STATURE

   iii. In FAVOR WITH GOD

   iv. In FAVOR WITH MAN

u.   When we next see Jesus, He is 30 years old, and being Baptized by John

LIFE OF CHRIST

A. Joseph—Jesus's step-father

    a. Bible ref—Matthew 1:18-2:23, Luke 1:26-38, 2:1-52, Luke 4:22

    b. Joseph of Nazareth—the MAN CHOSEN BY GOD TO PROVIDE PROTECTION AND NURTURING TO THE *SON OF GOD*

    c. Matthew 1—the genealogy of Joseph

        i. Was from Abraham

        ii. Was from tribe of Judah

        iii. Was from lineage of David

        iv. Fathers name was Jacob

        v. Husband of Mary

        vi. Matthew 1:19—Joseph is a *"Just Man"* or *"Righteous Man"* A Jewish man who adhered to the Law of Moses

        vii. A man who knew the Law, and the consequences of breaking it

    d. Matthew 1:19—Joseph was a *Loving Man*

        i. Not willing to make an example of Mary

        ii. Was going to put her away privately—divorce

        iii. Did not want her killed, which was the penalty of the Law

    e. Matthew 1:20—Joseph was a *Troubled Man*—He thought on the things that were happening in his life

    f. Matthew 1:24, Luke 2:4—Joseph was an *Obedient Man*

        i. FOUR times Joseph has dreams, and does what

        God tells him to do

1. v.24—Mary as his wife
2. 2:14—flight to Egypt
3. v.19—return to Israel
4. v.22—go to Galilee

    ii. He also went to Bethlehem to be taxed because the law of Rome said to (this was also to fulfill prophecy)

g. Joseph was a *Man who Listened*

h. Matthew 1:25—Joseph was a *Self-Controlled Man*

i. Joseph was a *Devout Man*

    i. Luke 2:41—to Jerusalem for the Feasts

    ii. Luke 4:16—Jesus in the Synagogue

    iii. Luke 2:21—Jesus being circumcised, and NAMED

    iv. Luke 2:22-24—offering the prescribed sacrifice

j. Joseph was a *Conscientious Man*

    i. Taught Jesus a trade—CARPENTER—Mark 6:3

    ii. Feared for family's safety—Matthew 2:22

    iii. Treated Jesus as his own son—Luke 3:23 (People considered Jesus to be Joseph's son)

k. Matthew 13:55—Joseph was a *CARPENTER* as well because the eldest son would as a rule follow in the father's footsteps----Carpenter was a very demanding job. Not only would you work with wood for building houses, but also would be a cabinetmaker, make farm implements, such as plows, ox yokes, etc. Would also be a wheelwright, as well as a cart maker. Also, would often just be cutting wood. Could also work with masonry and stone. Not just in "rural Nazareth," but also in the city of Sepphoris, about 5 miles from there. Would have been a *much-esteemed craftsman*

l. It is also assumed that Joseph was older than Mary, and that he died prior to Jesus starting His ministry, but again, this is only in traditions

m. Matthew 13:54-56, Mark 6:2-3—Joseph is a *Family Man*

    i. Had other sons:

        1. James

        2. Joses

        3. Simon

        4. Judas=Jude

    ii. Had daughters as well

LIFE OF CHRIST

MARY—The woman that God chose to be the Mother of Jesus

A. Mary would give Jesus his humanness

    a. Seed of the Woman—Genesis 3:15—through Adam sin came in, and it is through Christ that sin is finished.

    b. Virgin Birth—Isaiah 7:14—Matthew 1:18—child with the Holy Ghost, Luke 1:26-27

    c. JESUS WAS 100% GOD AND 100% MAN

B. Mary knew the prophecies of a MESSIAH, AND IT WAS THE HOPE OF EVERY YOUNG WOMAN TO BE THE MOTHER OF THE MESSIAH.

C. Mary was a very thoughtful woman

    d. Considers greeting of angel—Luke 1:28-29

    e. Mary ponders the shepherds—Luke 2:19

    f. Mary marvels at the words of Simeon—Luke 2:33

    g. Mary keeps the sayings of Jesus in her heart—Luke 2:51

D. Mary was an obedient woman

    h. Obedient to God—Luke 1:38

    i. Obedient to the Law—Luke 2:22-24

    j. Obedient to Joseph—Luke 2:4-5, Matthew 2:14-15

E. Mary was a motherly woman

    k. Worried about Jesus—Luke 2:41-51

    l. Faith in Jesus—John 2:3-5, and 12

    m. Came to see Jesus—Luke 8:19-21, Mark 3:31-35

      i. Some feel that Mark 3:21 is talking about His family,

but I don't think so

    n.   Stayed by her Son even to the end—John 19:25-27

F.   Mary was a devoted woman

    o.   With the disciples when Jesus ascended to heaven and later when they chose another disciple—Acts 1:12-14

    p.   Was probably with them on the day of Pentecost—Acts 2:1 vs. Act 1:14

G. Mary was a woman who recognized HER need for a savior—Luke 1:46-55➔ THE MAGNIFICANT

H. Mary was an incredibly humble woman

I.   MYTHS ABOUT MARY

    q.   She was also born a virgin birth

    r.   She was born in a cave in Jerusalem

    s.   She was a virgin her entire life—Matthew 13:55-56

    t.   She was the leader of the Church in Jerusalem

    u.   She rose from the dead on the third day

    v.   She ascended into Heaven

    w. She is interceding for us today with Jesus

    x.   She is "co-savior" with Jesus

LIFE OF CHRIST

A. John the Baptist

    a. Cousin of Jesus

    b. 6 months older than Jesus

    c. The final prophet of the Old Testament

        i. Matthew 11:13

        ii. Matthew 11:9

    d. Messenger sent to prepare the way

        i. Matthew 11:10

        ii. Malachi 3:1

        iii. Isaiah 40:3-4 (Luke 3:3-6)

    e. Gives a testimony of Jesus

        i. John 1:15-18

            1. V. 17

                a. "Law by Moses"

                b. "Grace and Truth by Jesus Christ"

        ii. "Behold the Lamb of God which taketh away the sin of the world"—John 1:29 and 36

    f. Message of John

    i. Matthew 3:2, Mark 1:4, Luke 3:3,

        1. Repent—turn away from doing wrong (sin)

        2. Kingdom of heaven is at hand—the Messiah is here!

        3. Forgiveness of sins—by a repentant attitude, and not doing the wrong stuff—Matthew 3:7-12, Luke 3:7-17

      ii.   John 1:19-27➔tells all that he (John) is not the Christ

  g. Baptism—from the Jewish Mikvaote—which were used for ceremonial cleansing

      i.   Priests would do this before entering the Temple to do duty

      ii.   Pilgrims would do this before bringing their sacrifices to the Temple

      iii.   Often this was part of the ritual of being clean from leprosy, etc.

      iv.   Proselytizers would do this to as a show of their converting to Judaism

  h. John is baptizing for the repentance from sin—as an outward sign that there is a change--same as our baptism today

  i. Jesus's baptism—Matthew, Mark and Luke all three have the *TRINITY* present, John shows it as after the baptism, and John the Baptist is saying that this was to be the sign that he would know--John 1:32-34

B. Jesus Christ

  j. Jesus about 30 years old Luke 3:23

  k. Comes to where John is baptizing Matthew 3:13, Mark 1:9

  l. Wants to be baptized, but John says, "No, I am not worthy." Mathew 3:14

  m. Jesus tells him to do it anyway Matthew 3:15

  n. TRINITY—IN ONE PLACE

      i.   Jesus the Son—Matthew 3:16, Mark 1:10, Luke 3:21

      ii.   The Holy Spirit—Matthew 3:16, Mark 1:10, Luke 3:22

     iii. God the Father—Matthew 3:17, Mark 1:11, Luke 3:22

o. Jesus then is "led"—Matthew 4:1 and Luke 4:1 or "driven"—Mark 1:12 into the wilderness--for what reason?

     i. Matthew 4:1—to be tempted of the devil (Mark 1:13 Luke 4:2)

     ii. Matthew 4:2—fasted 40 days and nights (Luke 4:2)

     iii. Mark 1:13—angels ministered to him (Matthew 4:11)

     iv. Mark 1:13—with the wild beasts

     v. Jesus is TEMPTED like we are, yet WITHOUT SIN—Hebrews 4:15

     vi. The TEMPTATIONS Matthew 4

         1. Physical—Jesus was hungry

             a. Able to meet his needs—by himself (not need help from God)

             b. Response—Man is not only physical, but also spiritual (Deuteronomy 8:3)

         2. Temporal—it was not time

             a. Where—Jerusalem, at the Temple

             b. What—through yourself down

             c. Why—prove that you are Christ

             d. Satan even used scripture—Psalms 91:11-12

             e. Response—do not tempt the Lord—God has everything in His time (Deuteronomy 6:16)

3. Spiritual—to have another instead of God

    a. These were Satan's to give as he wants

    b. Satan longs and desires that we worship him rather than God—this is accomplished by our placing *anything* in the way of God

    c. Response—Worship only God (Deuteronomy 6:13 and 10:20)

vii. Satan then leaves him— (for a season—Luke 4:13) Jesus defeated him with the WORD-*Scripture Ephesians 6:17*

viii. JESUS BEGAN HIS MINISTRY AFTER HIS "MOUNTAIN TOP" EXPERIENCE—THIS OFTEN IS ACCOMPANIED WITH AN AT-TACK FROM THE ENEMY"

ix. Matthew 4:17, Mark 1:15, Luke 4:14-21— "Repent for the Kingdom of Heaven is at hand"

LIFE OF CHRIST

A. Miracles

    a.   Jesus's ministry was only three years. During that time, He performed more miracles than in the entire Old Testament. His miracles were for the purpose of showing that He is God by his control over nature, healing of physical bodies, and the raising of the dead John 20:30-31. He also showed by the miracles that He cared about the needs of the people, from feeding a multitude to the paying of the Temple tax for Peter and Himself.

    b.   After Jesus Baptism by John, and being tempted by Satan, Jesus returned to Galilee and began to teach—

        i.   His message "Repent, for the Kingdom of Heaven is at hand" Matthew 4:17, Mark 1:15

        ii.   He became famous throughout the region—Luke 4:14-15, Matthew 4:23-25

    c.   The reading of Isaiah in the Synagogue—Luke 4:16-21

        i.   This was the regular reading for that day Isaiah 61:1-2

        ii.   Jesus only read the first half of verse two-*WHY* Jesus only read what was pertaining to the FIRST COMING—the rest of the verse will apply to the SECOND COMING

        iii.   Jesus *ADDED* to the verse with the recovery of sight—this is a Messianic Prophecy from Isaiah 35:4-6, Psalms 146:7-10

    d.   In Old Testament

        i.   Birth of Isaac, blindness of people

ii. Red Sea, Manna, quail, lasting of clothes and shoes (lasted for 40 years), sun standing still, water from the rock, healing from snake bite, walls of Jericho, Jordan River parting, Enemies killing each other, killing 1,000 with jawbone of an ass, amazing feats of strength, Elijah stopping rain, causing rain to fall, healing kings (Hezekiah) raising people from the dead, causing people to be blind and then to recover their sight, making iron swim, (Elisha and Elijah are about the last to perform these types of miracles) Hanukah, virgin birth, birth of John the Baptist.

e. Of Jesus

   i. Only a few are recorded for us in scripture-John 20:30-31

   ii. In Synagogue of Nazareth, he had already become famous before this. He did more personal miracles than before

   iii. Were others doing miracles as well, and Jesus said if they are not against them, then they are with him—Mark 9:38-40Jesus has given us the same ability, with the help of the Holy Spirit to do the same works, and greater—*Luke 10:19, John 14:12-14*

   iv. *ONE SPECIFIC ON MESSIAH➔HEALING THE BLIND*

   v. *Water into wine (John 2:1-11), raising the dead (Jairus's daughter, Widow's son, Lazarus),* healing the leper(s), casting out demons (into the pigs, many times from people), feeding the multitudes (5,000 and 4,000), *calming the storm (Matthew 8:23-27), walking on water (Matthew 14:25),* healing lame, healing woman with issue of blood Matthew 9:20-22), healing fever (Luke

4:38), healing crippled hand (Luke 6:6-10), healing the woman bent over (Luke 13:11-13), healing people from a distance (Mark 7:24-30, Luke 7:1-10), catching fish "out of time" (Luke 5:4-11, John 21:1-11), *deaf and mute (Matthew 9:32-33, Mark 7:31-37), BLIND (Matthew 9:27-31, Luke 18:35-43, Mark 8:22-26, John9:1-7)* , coin in fish (Matthew 17:24-27)

vi. Jesus is still in the business of miracles—He longs to show Himself real in our lives, just as He did 2000 years ago. It is often our faith that limits the miracles from happening to us. (Matthew 13:58, Mark 6:5-6)

LIFE OF CHRIST

The confession—Matthew 16:13-17, Mark 8:27-31, Luke 9:18-20, John 6:66-69

    a. Where—Caesarea Philippi—at the base of Mt. Hermon, where the Jordan River starts--was a center of pagan worship of Pan, the Greek god. (Modern name is Panius) There are niches carved in the rock for the statues and gifts given to Pan.

    b. Why—in answer to Jesus's question, "Who do men say that I am?"

        i. John the Baptist raised from the dead—teaching very much like John's

        ii. Elijah—to come before the Christ-Malachi 4:5

        iii. Jeremiah—announced the new covenant—Jeremiah 31:31-34

        iv. Other prophets

    c. Who do you say—Peter gives this answer

        i. The CHRIST➔the ANOINTED ONE

        ii. The Son of the Living GOD

    d. When—before the transfiguration

    e. By whom—Peter

        i. Jesus commends him for the Spiritual insight that he has➔*comes from God, not from himself*

        ii. It is Peter's CONFESSION that is the foundation of the Church, not Peter

    f. Keep it a secret until after Resurrection

A. The transfiguration—Matthew 17:1-19, Mark 9:2-10, Luke 9:28-36

g. VIEW OF THE KINGDOM OF GOD

h. What—Jesus taking on His glorified appearance

    i. Face—shine like the sun

    ii. Clothes—white as the light

i. Who—Jesus

j. Who else was there—six people

    i. Jesus

    ii. Moses—dead about 1700 years➔represents the completion of the Old Covenant➔completion/abolition of the Law

    iii. Elijah—not dead, but been living in heaven in earthly body for about 1000 years➔completion of the prophecies regarding the Messiah

        1. We have the representative of who is going to be in Heaven for ETER-NITY—will be the dead (Moses) and the translated (Elijah) *I Thessalonians 4:16-17*

        2. They are encouraging Jesus as He prepares for the Cross

        3. They confirm that Jesus is the *ONLY MEDIATOR BETWEEN GOD and MAN*

        4. Spoke about Jesus death in Jerusalem—Luke 9:31

    iv. Peter

    v. James

    vi. John

        1. The "inner circle" given this privilege

        2. Build them shelters or tabernacles to rest in

3. Hear the voice of GOD— "this is my beloved Son, in whom I am well pleased; hear ye Him"

4. Bright cloud overshadows them

5. Fall on their face and are afraid

   a. This should be our response when we encounter God

   b. Reverence and respect

k. Keep it a secret until He raises from the dead

B. Telling of his death—Matthew 16:21-22, 17:9-13, 17:22-23, 20:17-19, 20:27-28, Mark 8:31, Luke 9:21-22

l. Matthew 16:21

i. Must go to Jerusalem (Luke9:51)

ii. Suffer many things (Matthew 17:12, Luke 9:22)

iii. Suffering to be at the leadership

iv. Be killed (Luke 9:22)

v. Raise again the third day (Matthew 17:9)

m. Matthew 17:22-23

i. Jesus be betrayed

ii. Into the hands of MEN

iii. Will be killed

iv. Be raised again

n. Matthew 20:17-19

i. Go to Jerusalem

ii. Betrayed to priests

iii. Be condemned to death

iv. Mocked by Gentiles

v. Scourged

      vi. Crucified

      vii. Rise again

o. Matthew 20:28

      i. Give His life

      ii. Ransom for many

p. Luke 9:22

      i. Be rejected

q. A "Part II" of His ministry—Part I was repentance, but part II is to be salvation

LIFE OF CHRIST

A. TRIUMPHAL ENTRY—Mark 11:1-10 Matthew 21:8-11

    a. Palm Sunday—the general populace declare Jesus as the Messiah

    b. He is coming into the city as a king, not as a warrior--Zechariah 9:9

    c. Rides from Bethphage over the mount of olives, and into the Temple area

    d. Jesus does a lot of teaching in the few days after this.

        i. Cleansing of the Temple

        ii. Paying tribute to Caesar

        iii. Olivet discourse—prophecy about the future of Jerusalem, as well as the age we are in right now

B. JESUS ANOINTED AT BETHANY

    a. Reason—to prepare Him for his death--John 12:2-7, Mark 14:3-9, Matthew 26:6-13

    b. By—Mary, the sister of Lazarus John 11:2

C. THE LAST SUPPER

    a. A Passover Seder--retelling the Exodus and the deliverance of Israel from Egypt

    b. *JESUS CHANGED IT!*

    c. Judas leaves and gets the mob John 13:26-30

    d. Peter is told would deny Jesus

    e. Jesus does a lot of talking with the disciples--John 14:1-17:26

        i. Some of this is in Upper Room

        ii. Some as they are walking along through the Temple area

    f.   Subject—were many

        i.   Love

        ii.   Holy Spirit

        iii.   Persecution

        iv.   Relation of us to Him

D. GARDEN OF GETHSEMANE—Mark 14:32-42, 43-50

    a.   Place of solitude

    b.   Place of prayer

    c.   Asked the disciples to "keep watch and pray"

    d.   Surrenders to the will of the Father

    e.   BETRAYED BY JUDAS

    f.   Taken captive

    g.   Performs his last healing—John 18:10-11, Luke 22:50-51

E. HOUSE OF CAIAPHAS—Matthew 26:57-68

    a.   Caiaphas is the High Priest--also a prophet—John 11:49-52

    b.   Entire counsel is there

    c.   Bring false testimony against Jesus

    d.   JESUS SAYS NOTHING, UNTIL V.63-64

    e.   CHARGE--BLASPHEMY

    f.   Jesus is abused Luke 22:63-65

    g.   The leaders of the nation of Israel deny Christ

F. BEFORE PILATE—John 18:28-31

    a.   At daybreak

    b.   Jews would not go in, so Pilate had to come out

    c.   Jews couldn't kill Jesus because He had to be crucified

    d.   Pilate finds no reason to kill him

G. BEFORE HEROD—Luke 23:6-11

    a. Herod wanted to see some miracles

    b. Jesus did not answer

    c. Herod's troops abuse Him, then send Him to Pilate

    d. V. 12—Pilate and Herod become friends

H. BEFORE PILATE

    a. Jesus given to Roman soldiers

        i. Scourge Him

        ii. Crown of thorns

        iii. Purple robe—from Herod or a new one, not sure

    b. Jesus brought back out—John 19:5

    c. Jesus then taken to be crucified

I. TO GOLGOTHA

    a. Jesus is killed

    b. Stabbed with spear

    c. Centurion's confession—Matthew 27:54

J. BURRIED IN JOSEPH'S TOMB—Matthew 27:57-61, Mark 15:42-47, Luke 23:50-56, John 19:38-42

    a. Joseph and Nicodemus

    b. Followed Jewish burial practices of the time

K. JESUS ROSE FROM THE DEAD

    a. HE IS NOT HERE, BUT HE IS RISEN

L. JESUS ASCENDED TO HEAVEN Acts 1:9

M. JESUS IS COMING BACK Acts 1:11

LEVEL 3

Seeker of Comfort

But the Comforter, which is the Holy Ghost
John 14:26

I will pray the Father and he shall give you another Comforter,
that he may abide with you forever.
John 14:16

But ye shall receive power after that the Holy Ghost
Is come upon you
Acts 1:8

BAPTISM IN THE HOLY SPIRIT

A. When a person accepts Jesus as their Lord and Savior, they are given a measure of the Holy Spirit. This is what draws us to God in the first place and convicts us of sin. This is where many stop. However, as Pentecostals, we believe in the "Baptism of the Holy Spirit," which makes us different from other churches.

B. The baptism of the Holy Spirit is for all believers.

   a. It is subsequent to salvation

   b. It is distinct from salvation Acts 8:12-17

   c. It follows the new birth experience Acts 19:2-6

   d. It continues the work of spiritual growth begun at salvation

C. It is a promise from God Luke 24:49 Luke 11:13

   a. It is available to all believers

      i. Are all *entitled* to receive Acts 2:4

      ii. It is for everyone Joel 2:28

   b. We must ask for it, and believe *(expect)* that we will receive it *(earnestly seek)*

   c. The Baptism of the Holy Spirit provides us with what we need to work for God (Kingdom)

      i. Power—this power is from God—Luke 24:46-49 Acts 1:8

      ii. Glory to God—as we witness, we tell of Jesus through our *lives*, our **words**, and our *works*

   d. Who is the Holy Spirit—He is God-third person of the

Trinity

   i. A person—He speaks, is grieved, witnesses, commands, and forbids, aids in prayer, gives council, reveals the mysteries of God.

   ii. Guide—guides and directs our steps John 16:13

   iii. Teacher—teaches us what to say John 14:26

   iv. Reminder—John 14:26

   v. Advocate or Comforter—John 14:16

   vi. Helper—Romans 8:26

   vii. Revealer—1 Corinthians 2:10

   viii. Transformer—2 Corinthians 3:18

   ix. Spirit of God—Ephesians 4:30

   x. Spirit of Christ—Romans 8:9

   xi. Spirit of Truth—John 14:17

   xii. Source of Power—Zechariah 4:6, Acts 1:8

   xiii. Convicts us of Sin—John 16:8-11

   xiv. Glorifier of Christ—John 16:14-15

e. Our experience following the Baptism

   i. An overflowing fullness of the Spirit—John 7:37-39

   ii. Reverence for God—Acts 2:43

   iii. Commitment to God and His work—Acts 2:42

   iv. Deeper love for Christ, His word, and evangelism—Mark 16:20

   v. Desire to share the Gospel—Acts 1:8

   vi. Understanding of the Word of God—1 Corinthians 2:16

f. Following Baptism of Holy Spirit, Gifts of the Spirit are given by God to operate within the Church 1 Corinthians 12:1-31

    i. Wisdom

    ii. Knowledge

    iii. Faith

    iv. Healing

    v. Miracles

    vi. Prophecy

    vii. Discerning of spirits

    viii. Tongues

    ix. Interpretation of tongues

    x. These gifts are for the spread of the gospel, as well as the Church. Hebrews 2:3-4, Mark 16:20

g. Following the Baptism of the Holy Spirit, the Fruit of the Spirit will begin to be apparent in one's life Galatians 5:22-23 2 Corinthians 3:18

    i. Love

    ii. Joy

    iii. Peace

    iv. Longsuffering

    v. Gentleness

    vi. Goodness

    vii. Faith

    viii. Meekness

    ix. Temperance

INITIAL EVIDENCE OF BAPTISM IN HOLY SPIRIT

A. Speaking in other (unlearned) tongues Acts 2:4, Mark 16:17-18

B. God gives the ability—is not something we have learned

C. This is separate from salvation

D. Tongues is a manifestation of the Holy Spirit—Acts 2:4, I Corinthians 14:14-15

E. Tongues are the INITIAL outward sign of the baptism in the Holy Spirit—Acts 2:4, Acts 10:45-46, Acts 19:6

F. Tongues as a gift—to Church and to each believer

    a. Gift of the Holy Spirit—I Corinthians 12:4-10

        i. Used with gift of interpretation

        ii. Must have understanding to edify entire church—I Corinthians 14:2-4, 18-19

    b. Used by the *believer* to speak to God in personal devotions

        i. Praying—I Corinthians 14:2, 14, 28

        ii. Giving thanks—I Corinthians 14:16-17

        iii. Singing—I Corinthians 14:15

    c. Holy Spirit should be a normal part of our personal worship—Ephesians 5:14-20, Mark 16:17

LEVEL 4

Seeker of Guidance

All scripture is given by inspiration of God,
and is profitable for doctrine, for reproof, for correction, for
instruction in righteousness
2ⁿᵈ Timothy 3:16

Thy word have I hid in mine heart,
that I might not sin against thee
Psalm 119:11

Thy word is a lamp unto my feet, and a light unto my path.
Psalm 119:105

THE BIBLE

Some of the false ideas about the Bible

1. Just a book like any other book

2. A book of myths and folk tales

3. A "religious" book

4. A fictitious book that tells a group of ancient "Jewish" legends

5. Collection of myths that have been elaborated to try to prove the existence of a "mythical Christ figure"

6. Group of anti-Semitic writings to explain the hatred of the Jews

Truths of the Bible

1. Bible is a work of God, not men

2. All of the events of the Bible are FACT

3. A book about a LOVING RELATIONSHIP, not Religion

4. Tells the FACTS of the History of the Jewish People

5. Presents Jesus Christ as the Savior of the World, and the only way to God

6. Shows a loving, caring relationship between God and the Jews, (and us)

What we believe about the BIBLE

1. The Bible is Inspired—the scriptures of the entire Bible are verbally inspired of God. It was not just the ideas that were inspired, but even the choice of words were inspired as the original writers were moved by God to write what HE wanted them to say.

2. We believe that the Scriptures are God's revelation of

73

Himself to mankind.

3. We believe they are infallible (NEVER WRONG).

    1. We believe they are the divinely authoritative guide for our faith, belief, and manner of living (II Timothy 3:16-17)

    2. IF THIS IS NOT THE CASE, THEN WE HAVE NO STANDARD ON WHICH TO BASE OUR LIVES. (If our foundation is not there, then what are we to build on?)

WHO WROTE THE BIBLE?

1. Bible written by GOD, not by men (I Corinthians 2:13-14, II Peter 1:20-21, II Timothy 3:15-17, I Thessalonians 2:13)

2. God used men as the instruments for writing, but it is all the HEART and MIND of God

3. It is God's Love Letter to US, His Children

4. It explains how We can have a loving Relationship with a Holy God

5. IS NOT WRITTEN BY MEN!

WHAT THE BIBLE IS *NOT*

A. NOT A HISTORY BOOK—but where it has history it has been proven to be correct

B. NOT A SCIENCE BOOK—but where speaks about scientific things it has always been correct

C. NOT A BOOK OF MORALS—but if it is applied to our lives, it brings morality to a society

It is the only book in the world where the author is immediately available to guide us in understanding it as we read it. It is the only book in the world that when you attempt to practice its

teachings, the author is there to give you the strength and grace you need. *

BIBLE DIVISIONS

A. Bible is made up of 66 books

B. Divided into two parts

    a. Old Testament➜made up of 39 books

        i. Divided into 5 categories

           1. LAW—Torah

           2. HISTORY—Joshua – Esther

           3. POETRY—Job-Song of Solomon

           4. MAJOR PROPHETS—Isaiah-Daniel

           5. MINOR PROPHETS—Hosea-Malachi

        ii. In Jewish Bible, there are fewer books because often the books of Samuel, Kings and Chronicles are just one book rather than two books

    b. New Testament➜made up of 27 books

        i. Divided into 5 categories

           1. GOSPELS—Matthew-John

           2. HISTORY—Acts

           3. PAULINE EPISTLES—Romans-Hebrews

           4. GENERAL EPISTLES—James-Jude

           5. PROPHECY—Revelation

C. WHAT IS THE COMMON THEME THROUGH THE ENTIRE BIBLE?

    a. LOVE OF GOD TO US

    b. GOD WANTING A RELATIONSHIP WITH US

    c. BLOOD ATONEMENT FOR SIN

    d. SIN WILL BE PUNISHED

    e.   EVIL WILL BE PUT AWAY FOR GOOD

    f.   LIVE WITH GOD ETERNALLY

D. GOD'S WORD IS: Hebrews 4:12

    a.   Quick

    b.   Powerful

    c.   Sharp

    d.   Discerner of our sin

E. We are to desire the Word of God. It makes us:

    a.   Psalms 1:1-3

    b.   Psalms 19:7-11

    c.   Psalms 119:1-176

THE BIBLE

Some of the false ideas about the Bible

1. Just a book like any other book
2. A book of myths and folk tales
3. A "religious" book
4. A fictitious book that tells a bunch of myths about "Christian" ideals
5. A bunch of anti-Semitic writings to teach hatred of the Jews

Bible written by God, not men

1. II Peter 1:20-21
2. II Timothy 3:15-17
3. I Thessalonians 2:13

God used men as instruments for writing, but it is HIS words it shows:

1. The HEART OF GOD
2. The MIND OF GOD
3. The LOVE OF GOD

*It is the only book in the world where the author is immediately available to guide us in understanding it as we read it. It is the only book in the world that when you attempt to practice its teaching, the author is there to give you the strength and grace you need. *

New Testament--made up of 27 books

Divided into 5 categories

1. GOSPELS—Matthew-John

2. HISTORY—Acts

3. PAULINE EPISTLES—Romans-Hebrews

4. GENERAL EPISTLES—James-Jude

5. PROPHECY—Revelation

Gospels--they tell the story of JESUS, the Son of God--John 20:30-31, Luke 1:1-4

Acts--the history of the new church, starting with Pentecost and then going into the ministry of Apostles and Paul

Pauline Epistles--letters written by Paul to churches and to individuals➜Peter considered them along with all scripture II Peter 3:15-16

General Epistles--letters written by others for instruction and exhortation—written by the Apostles and leaders in the church mostly warning against those who would pervert the Gospel

Revelation--is the only book of prophecy in the New Testament, but it is not the only prophecy in that portion of the Book: Jesus as well as Paul spoke a lot about the "End Times," and about the deception that would come about.

Revelation is the last book of the Bible. *It is complete.* There are no new books or revelations from God. We have the entire Bible, the Old and New Testaments, both of which are inspired by GOD, and we have the HOLY SPIRIT to guide us in understanding it➜John 16:13, John 14:26

The BIBLE is completely trustworthy and does not change ➜

John 17:17, Psalms 12:6-7, Isaiah 40:8, Luke 21:33

"The new is in the Old concealed; the Old is in the New revealed."

We use the Bible for: II Timothy 3:16-17, I John 5:13, I Corinthi-

ans 10:11-12, Romans 15:4, John 20:31

Our ENEMY, Satan does not want us to get into the Word--he will do everything possible to keep us from the word, even to changing or twisting the word and making it weak and ineffective. (Satan knows the Bible, and he quotes it to cause us to fall.)

Our TASK is to get into the Word and let the Word get into Us-- Psalms 119:11, 105, 133, Proverbs 6:20-23

THE BIBLE

We have the entire Bible as God intended it to be. There are no new books being added to it, such as the Book of Mormon, the Koran, or any other book that try to be added. →Revelation 22:18-19—"For I testify unto every man that heareth the words of the prophecy of this book, if any man shall add unto these things, God shall add unto him the plagues that are written in this book: V. 19 And if any man shall take away from the words of the book of this prophecy, God shall take away his part out of the book of life, and out of the holy city, and from the things which are written in this book."

The Bible is trustworthy and does not change

1. John 17:17--it is TRUTH— "Sanctify them through thy truth: thy word is truth."

2. Psalms 12:6-7--it is PURE and PRESERVED— "The words of the LORD are pure words: as silver tried in a furnace of earth, purified seven times. V. 7 Thou shalt keep them, O LORD, thou shalt preserve them from this generation forever."

3. Isaiah 40:8--it will stand FOREVER (ETERNAL)— "The grass withereth, the flower fadeth, but the word of our God shall stand for ever."

4. Luke 21:33--it is ETERNAL— "Heaven and earth shall pass away: but my words shall not pass away."

5. Matthew 5:18--it is ETERNAL— "For verily I say unto you, Till heaven and earth pass, one jot or one tittle shall in no wise pass from the law, till all be fulfilled."

6. Psalms 119:89--it is ETERNAL— "Forever, O LORD, thy word is settled in heaven."

The Bible is our guide in living

1. II Timothy 3:16-17--it is our guide for DOCTRINE, REPROOF, CORRECTION, and INSTRUCTION— "All scripture is given by inspiration of God, and is profitable for doctrine, for reproof, for correction, for instruction in righteousness: V. 17 That the man of God may be perfect, thoroughly furnished unto all good works."

2. I John 5:13--these are so we KNOW we have ETER- NAL LIFE— "These things have I written unto you that believe on the name of the Son of God: that ye may know that ye have eternal life, and that ye may believe on the name of the Son of God."

3. I Corinthians 10:11-12--these are EXAMPLES in how to LIVE and NOT live— "Now all these things hap- pened unto them for ensamples: and they are written for our admonition, upon whom the ends of the world are come. V. 12 Wherefore let him that thinketh he standeth take heed lest he fall."

4. Romans 15:4--for us to LEARN and have HOPE and COMFORT— "For whatsoever things were writ- ten aforetime were written for our learning, that we through patience and comfort of *the scriptures* might have hope."

5. John 20:31--that we can BELIEVE on JESUS and have LIFE— "But these are written, that ye might be- lieve that Jesus is the Christ, the Son of God; and that believing ye might have life through his name."

6. Psalms 119:9--tells how to keep our LIVES CLEAN— "Wherewithal shall a young man cleanse his way? By taking heed thereto according to thy word."

7. Psalms 119:11--it KEEPS US FROM SINNING— "Thy word have I hid in mine heart, that I might not sin against thee."

8. Psalms 1:1-3--it keeps us SAFE, and we are PROS-PEROUS— "Blessed is the man that walketh not in the counsel of the ungodly, nor standeth in the way of sinners, nor sitteth in the seat of the scornful. V. 2 But his delight is in the law of the LORD; and in his law doth he meditate day and night. V. 3 And he shall be like a tree planted by the rivers of water, that bringeth forth his fruit in his season; his leaf also shall not wither; and whatsoever he doeth shall prosper.

Satan, our enemy, *hates* the Bible, and will do everything he can to *TWIST, DESTROY, WATER DOWN, AND MAKE IT INEFECTIVE.* How has he done this?

1. PEOPLE WILL CORRUPT THE WORD OF GOD

    a. II Corinthians 2:17— "For we are not as many, which corrupt the word of God: but as of sincerity, but as of God, in the sight of God speak we in Christ."

    b. Matthew 24:11— "And many false prophets shall rise and shall deceive many."

    c. II Peter 2:1-3— "But there were false prophets also among the people, even as there shall be false teachers among you, who privily shall bring in damnable heresies, even denying the LORD that bought them, and bring upon themselves swift destruction. V. 2 And many shall follow their pernicious ways; by reason of whom the way of truth shall be evil spoken of. V. 3 *And through covetousness shall they with feigned words make merchandise of you*: whose judgment now of a long time lingereth not, and their damnation slumbereth not.

2. SATAN IS THE AUTHOR OF CONFUSSION, NOT GOD

a. I Corinthians 14:33— "For God is not the author of confusion, but of peace, as in all churches of the saints."

b. *EXAMPLE*➔*Mark 1:1-2*

3. SATAN HAS HAD MANY VERSES OMITED FROM THE BIBLE, INCLUDING VERSES OF BASIC DOCTRINE

   a. Mark 16:9-20--THIS IS THE RESURECTION OF JESUS!

   b. I John 5:7➔THIS IS THE TRINITY

   c. I John 5:13, Acts 8:37➔THIS IS TO BELIEVE IN JESUS AS SAVIOR

   d. Luke 9:56, Matthew 18:11➔THIS IS THE REDEMPTIVE WORK OF JESUS

   e. I Timothy 3:16, Revelation 1:8-13➔THIS IS THE DIETY OF JESUS

   f. Romans 14:10-12➔THIS IS JESUS AS THE ULTIMATE JUDGE

   g. Acts 3:13, Acts 3:26, John 6:69➔THIS IS JESUS AS THE "SON OF GOD"

   h. Luke 2:33, 34, Matthew 1:25➔THIS IS THE DOCTRINE OF THE VIRGIN BIRTH OF JESUS

   i. Mark 13:33, Mark 9:29, Matthew 17:21➔THIS IS ABOUT FASTING

   j. Luke 11:2, Matthew 6:13➔THIS IS THE LORD'S PRAYER

Satan has done everything he can to destroy man. In the late 1800's he brought in two new "ideas" for man, a new science with EVOLUTION by Charles Darwin (1859 *Origin of a Species*) and a new Bible the Greek text based on Vaticanus and Sinaiticus by Hort and Westcott (1853). Their work has been the backbone of every "modern" translation starting in 1881 with the Revised Version. The Authorized Version used a different Greek, the Textus Receptus or Received Text. The translators had access to the Vaticanus and other forms, but they rejected them because of errors regarding doctrine. We can see why this is. The NIV is the most "nondenominational" Bible in print. You can prove or disprove anything just with the same Bible. THIS SHOULD NOT BE. The NIV is much like the New World Translation made up by the Jehovah Witnesses. In fact, if you were to use a NIV to witness to them, they may just bring out a NIV to witness to you. HOW CAN THIS BE? Yet Satan is doing all he can to bring the "DAMNABLE HERESIES" into the church, and he is SUCCEEDING.

LEVEL 5

Seeker of a Hero

Now these things were our examples
1ˢᵗ Corinthians 10:6

*Now all these things happened unto them
for examples*
1ˢᵗ Corinthians 10:11

*Because Christ also suffered for us,
leaving us an example, that ye
should follow his steps*
1ˢᵗ Peter 2:21

WHAT IS "FAITH?"

Hebrews 11:1-2

People of Faith—Jews, Islam, Christians.

What is the Jewish "faith" looking for? A Messiah, a "Home land," a new way of life, rest and peace.

What are the people of Islam looking for? A reward when they die, but there is no assurance of this.

What about the Christian?

"being sure of what we hope for" What is that for the Christian?

Healing—1 Peter 2:24

Salvation—2 Timothy 3:14-15

Resurrection –1 Corinthians 15

Eternal Life—John 6:47

Heaven—John 14:2

"Certain of what we do not see" What about Christians?

Spiritual Warfare—2 Corinthians 10:4, Ephesians 6:12

Jesus—John 20:29

Unseen, or out of reach?

Not really because that is the hope.

Where is the hope for Islam, Reincarnation, Animists, etc.

Who in the Bible is commended for their faith—

By Jesus—Primarily Gentiles

Centurion—Matthew 8:10, Luke 7:9

Phoenician Woman—Matthew 15:28

Friends of paralytic—Mark 2:5

People who were healed Luke 17:19, Luke 8:48, Matthew 9:22, etc.

By Paul—Timothy—2 Timothy 1:5

>   Church in Rome—Romans 1:8

>   Church in Ephesus—Ephesians 1:15

>   Church in Philippi—Philippians 1:25

>   Church in Colossae—Colossians 1:4-5

>   Church in Thessalonica—1 Thessalonians 1:8

>   And many others.

Who is reprimanded for their lack of faith?

>   By Jesus—Disciples—Matthew 8:26, Matthew 14: 31, Matthew 17:20

>   Town of Nazareth—Matthew 13:57-58

We must have faith in order to please God. —Hebrews 11:6

Questions that arose about faith:

1.   Can faith be damaged or "decreased"-what if you pray for something specific, and it does not happen—so do we then not trust God?

2.   Can we question our faith, or that of other?

>   How can we help others to grow in their faith?

>   How can we encourage one another in the faith?

>   If we are to do this, then we are *not* to discourage them.

>   What about teaching that denies miracles, or the things of God?

3.   Do we limit God because our faith is limited? --Romans 3:3-4

>   Disciples asked why they could not do this. Mat-

thew 17:19.

Are we "Empty Vessels" that God can fill, use, mold or break?

4. Are we cautious about "stepping out in faith" or "taking a leap of faith"?

Do we limit our faith because of "logic?"

Do we "reason" ourselves out of a blessing or "talk" ourselves out of a miracle?

The opposite of faith is doubting. Matthew 21:21, Mark 11:22-26, James 1:6, *Jude 20-22.*

What are we to do with our faith?

1. Our faith rests in God, not in men. 1 Corinthians 2:4-5

2. We are to grow in our faith. 2 Thessalonians 1:3, Philippians 1:25

3. We are to try or test our faith (or rather God does) James 1:3

4. We are to be established in our faith. Acts 16:5

5. We are to increase our faith, (exercise). 2 Corinthians 10:14

6. We are to live by faith. Galatians 2:20

7. Size of our faith—Mustard seed. Matthew 17:20, Luke 17:5-6

8. We are to have joy in our faith. Philippians 1:25

9. We are to encourage one another in the faith. 1 Thessalonians 3:2-3

Our actions show our faith.

Hebrews 11:3-7

Faith must be anchored in or on something.

Hebrews 11:3

What is the first thing we have to accept by faith?

Creation—what is the basis for the Christians faith that God created the universe? Genesis 1:1

Two explanations for the universe

1. speculation

2. revelation

Faith rests upon the Word of God. (The word became flesh and dwelt among us.)

Three examples of faith before the flood.

1. The way of Faith—Able.

2. The walk of Faith—Enoch.

3. The witness of Faith—Noah.

Hebrews 11:4 the way of Faith-- Able

The story of Able is in Genesis 4:1-10.

What caused the difference between Cain and Able?

1. Genetics

2. Environment

3. Sin

They brought an offering unto the Lord. Both brought something, from their livelihood, but Cain was rejected where Able was accepted.

1. Attitude—Cain seems to have a chip on his shoulder about it. I think that Adam told them what God expected, and I think that God himself did as well. Faith comes by hearing, and hearing by the Word of God. (Romans 10:17) Both of them had the same chance, to do right. Yet Cain rejected it even a second time (Genesis 4:7)

2. Motives –Was Cain coming with works? Was it because *HE* had grown them? Even if they were the best, was he trying to get it done on works?

3. The type of offering—what was it to be? It had to be a lamb or some other animal. God had shown that to Adam and Eve.

Abel's offering was pointing to Christ, the Lamb of God, and he came by *FAITH.*

Christ even calls Able righteous (Matthew 23:35)

Hebrews 11:5 the walk of Faith—Enoch

The story of Enoch is in Genesis 5:18-24

What is so special about Enoch?

1. Son of Jared—Jared means to descend- could be a testimony of the condition of things at that time.

2. Enoch means dedicated. He was dedicated to God.

3. Enoch came to "walk with God" after the birth of Methuselah. What caused this change in his life??? Was it the birth of his son?

4. Enoch walked with God. He was in close fellowship with God and was an example to those around him. He walked by *FAITH, not* by rules and regulations. His walk was pleasing to God.

5. Enoch was a prophet. Jude 14-15

6. Enoch was not. He was not found. He vanished. Can you imagine the search party that must have occurred? *We need to live such a life, that when we are gone, we will be missed.*

7. God took him. Enoch was translated, or raptured. This means to remove from one place to another. *Could this have been what would have happened to Adam and Eve and their descendants if they had not sinned?*

8. Two lessons we can get from Enoch.

    a. The peril of being influenced by our surroundings.

    b. The peril of thinking it is too hard to live for God.

    c. We have so much that they did not, such as the Word, Christ, etc.

We cannot please God without faith. When we come to him, we must believe two things:

1. That God Exists.

2. That God Rewards those who seek Him.

A WITNESS OF FAITH—NOAH

Story of Noah is in Genesis 5:28-10:1. Hebrews 11:7

Noah was the tenth from Adam.

The name of Noah means "comfort" in that they would have rest or comfort from the toil that they were doing to live.

Noah is called by God during a time when there is no one following God.

The man Noah

1. Righteous

   The only one at that time. God will always have a witness. That is what Noah was to the world at this time. The one who was right was Noah (Ezekiel 14:14) His house was saved because of his witness.

2. Blameless

   Noah was a preacher of righteousness (2 Peter2: 5).

3. Walked with God

   Noah and Enoch are the only two people who are described this way before the flood. No one else in scripture is referred to by this phrase

Noah found *GRACE* in the eyes of the Lord.

This is the first time that Grace is mentioned in scripture.

Grace is unmerited favor or undeserved favor.

Noah followed God's plan to the letter.

He did not question God

Another example of FAITH and OBEDIENCE going together.

Saved all of creation that lived on the earth from the flood.

Saved his own household.

It seems that worship and communication changed from the flood on.

1. Now there is Grace.

2. Here is the first *"alter"* built for worship.

    a. Why

        1. Now to worship in a specific place.

        2. As a memorial to some event or deliverance that God has done in a person's life. The rest of the Old Testament seems to support this.

    b. Also, it seems to be a place where people would gather, rather than hear God speak directly to their own conscience. Here is the start of Human Government.

3. First time that animals are divided into two categories, that of being clean and unclean.

    Would this be a refinement of the sacrificial animals???

4. This seems to be the point where there is a greater separation between God and Man.

5. Meat is now added to man's diet. (Genesis 9:3-4) This could have to do with spiritual warfare.

Noah was a *witness* of Faith.

1. God's judgment is plain and is told to Noah in Genesis 6:13.

2. Noah is given a job to do for the <u>salvation </u>of his house, and I think anyone who would have listened to him.

3. We often think that Noah preached for over 100 years, and did not make any converts, but we forget about his family.

4. We are to be a *witness* of our Faith.

   1. God's judgment is plain, and we are told about it in scripture.

   2. We are given a job to do for the <u>salvation</u> of our house, and anyone who listens to us.

   3. We must not forget about our families.

   4. Our time is compared to Noah's time by Christ in Matthew 24:37-39.

      a. Living life as if nothing is going to happen.

      b. Unaware of impending judgment.

      c. Guilty of apathy in the Church.

How can we have the same testimony that Noah had?

1. Listening to and obeying the Holy Spirit.

2. Reading the Word of God.

3. Claiming the Promises of God.

4. Get "in tune" or "same wavelength" as God.

What evidence would there be if we were to "walk with God?"

1. We would walk according to the spirit, not by flesh.

2. Be obedient to the Word.

3. We would be "heavenly minded"

4. We would have a desire to please our Heavenly

Father.

5. We would see people as Jesus sees them, people who are lost and in need of a Savior.

We are to be an example to the world by showing the WAY of faith, as Able, by doing the WALK of faith like Enoch, and being a WITNESS of faith like Noah.

Lessons to learn from Noah:

1. God always judges the wicked.

2. God blesses those who believe on him, not just the "good" people.

3. Noah was:

   a. Righteous man

   b. Builder of the ark

   c. A preacher of righteousness

   d. Elected

   e. Protected

   f. Delivered

   g. Remembered by God

ABRAHAM, A WORSHIP OF FAITH. HEBREWS 11:8-19

A. Life before God

   1. His father and family were pagans. (Joshua 24:2)

   2. Most likely Abraham and Sarah were also pagan.

B. Abraham is very family oriented. When he hears from God, he begins to move, and so does his family.

   1. Lot—his nephew goes along with them.

   2. Sarah—his wife and half-sister.

   3. Terah—his father.

   4. His family later.

      i. Lot—they have to part to maintain peace in the family.

      ii. Ishmael—is sent away.

         1. Abraham longed for him to follow God. (Genesis 17:18) God makes plain that the promise is through Isaac. In fact, God even gives the name of the offspring before he was born. (Genesis

17:19)

    2. He does however obtain the blessing from God.

iii. Isaac—to be sacrificed out of *obedience*.

iii. His other children.

    1. These are all sent away with gifts.

    2. All that he has goes to Isaac.

How important are our families to us? Are we willing to leave all that is familiar and go where God calls us to go? Are we willing to "stand out" in order to win them?

C. Abraham's call is before his father's death. (Genesis 12:1)

    1. He obeyed by *FAITH* and left his family, his country, and all that was familiar to him, and went to a place he did not know.

    2. God was to be the guide.

    3. When he gets to the Promised Land, God again gives the same promise, to give this land to his offspring. THERE WERE NONE AT THIS TIME. It takes FAITH when there are no children to claim that promise.

    4. We see a life of FAITH, trusting in divine guidance, believing in divine promises.

D. Abraham builds an alter and worships when God speaks to him.

E. He was an alien and stranger in this land. Was look-
    ing for a city that was permanent and built by God.
    Lived in tents. This would take faith to not even
    make a place of permanence. (In fact, the only place
    he bought was for the buying of his wife and later
    the rest of the family.)

    1. An alien is someone who does
        not belong or is not a native.

    2. No record of anyone having a
        permanent dwelling until get to
        Egypt, where they were slaves.

    3. A city with foundations—a per-
        manent place. Hebrews 11:10

        i. Builder is God. Jesus said
           he was going to make a
           place for us.

        ii. Architect is also God. His
           design is perfect.

    4. They could have returned to their
        old country if they had wanted to
        but kept looking for a heavenly
        one. (Hebrews 11:15-16)

    5. God is not ashamed to be called
        their God.

    Are we setting a good example of who God is?
    Is he pleased with us calling Him our God?

F. Abraham and Sarah both have the faith to have a
    son. Hebrews 11:11 Imagine the way they must have
    tried, even to the extent of having Ishmael.

    1. Yet they had faith to try again,
        after the promise of God that in
        HIS TIME the event would take
        place.

2. Abraham was as good as dead (Hebrews 11:12)

3. Sarah was past childbearing age, yet it was through FAITH that she was able to conceive.

4. Both had faith that they would be a family.

G. By faith he lost his family.

1. It grieved him to send Ishmael away.

2. Had to offer up Isaac as a sacrifice. In his mind, the young man was already dead. He had "determined" it in his heart to do what God asked.

3. He had faith that God could raise him from the dead. (Hebrews 11:17-19) *And God did.*

Are we willing to "surrender" all that we have and trust God? God will often take it and give it back to us. Are we willing to leave our "comfort zone" and go or do what God calls us to do? Do we have the faith to trust him with our futures, as well as our pasts?

H. BY FAITH HE GAVE ALL HE HAD TO ISAAC. He was the son of Promise.

I. Abraham married after Sarah's death and had other children, and they also became nations as well.

J. He died at 175 years old, had 8 children, and was buried by Isaac and Ishmael next to Sarah in Hebron.

Abraham is called a "Friend of God." We need to consider the cost of following God. It could cost us our families, our fortunes, all we hold dear to give it up for a relationship with God.

We are to also be a chosen people. We are to be holy, and our works are to go before us.

ISAAC—A WILLINGNESS OF FAITH.

Story of Isaac is in Genesis 17-27, Hebrews 11:20.

Isaac is born when Abraham is 100, and Sarah is 91. (Genesis 17:17- 21)

His name means "to laugh or the laughing one."

God foretells Isaac's birth, and the name is given before he is born. He is one if only a few to have that happen.

We know of his being circumcised when he was 8 days old. (This is in accordance to the covenant God made with Abraham.)

He is weaned, and there is a celebration. This results in Hagar and Ishmael being sent away.

In Isaac, we see someone who is *willing* to do what God wants him to do.

1. Was willing when Abraham offered him up as a sacrifice.

   a. Submission to the will of his father and his father's God.

   b. Probably 25-33 years old when this occurred.

   c. Only asked one question—where is the lamb?

2. Submissive when his father selected a wife for him.

   a. Did not want a Canaanite wife for Isaac. Do not be unequally yoked.

   b. Rebekah was Isaac's cousin.

   c. His wife comforted him after death of his mother.

     d.   Isaac loved Rebekah.

     e.   He was 40 years old when he got married.

3.   He lived in tents, just like his father. Waiting for a city.

4.   Extremely wealthy. Abraham had left everything to him.

5.   *He and Ishmael* bury Abraham next to Sarah in the place he had bought for that purpose. (There is still that family bond, but it goes downhill very fast after this.)

Isaac interceded for his wife when she was barren. In order for the promise to be fulfilled, there would have to be offspring. Isaac was 60 when the twins were born. (He had been waiting 20 years. You wonder if he did not want to make the same mistake and get another Ishmael.)

1.   Isaac and Rebekah had favorite sons.

2.   Each twin was very different.

3.   Isaac knew that there was a prophecy regarding Jacob and Esau.

     a.   *They would be two nations.*

     b.   *The older would serve the younger.*

4.   Isaac tries to give a blessing to Esau but gives it to Jacob instead.

5.   Isaac sends Jacob away to get a wife, because does not want him to marry a Canaanite wife like Esau had done. (Esau hears about it and decides to marry a cousin from Ishmael.)

Isaac went to all the places that Abraham went, and re-dug the wells. He gave up several because of disputes. Finally, there was enough room. (Is this the first "Land for Peace" in Israel?)

"BY FAITH ISAAC BLESSED JACOB AND ESAU REGUARDING THE FUTURE."

He recognized the blessings and did go ahead and put the older second. (This is a trend in the Bible, about the second getting it right, and the blessing, and the "first shall be last and the last shall be first.")

He died at 180 years old, and Esau and Jacob buried him in Hebron, next to Abraham and Sarah. (The reconciliation of Esau and Jacob. God is a god of reconciliation.)

What do we learn?

1. God always does what He promises.

2. We need to be obedient to God. That FAITH AND OBEDIENCE thing.

3. God has our best interest in mind, even if we do not see it.

JACOB—A FAITH THAT SUSTAINED HIM.

Genesis 27-35, Genesis 46-49, Hebrews 11:21.

His name means "supplanter" or deceiver. It also means taking the place of another.

Jacob-a twin with promise. (Genesis 25:23)

1. Esau—a hunter, the favorite of his father,

    a. An outdoorsman.

    b. Married to two Canaanite women.

        i. These were a source of grief to Isaac and Rebekah.

        ii. Married when he was 40 years old. (Genesis 26:34-35)

    c. Married a daughter of Ishmael.

        i. Mahalath was her name.

        ii. He realized how his other marriages upset his father. (Genesis 28:6-9)

    d. A man of the world. Wanted instant gratification, so willing to sell his birthright for a bowl of soup. (Genesis 25:29-34)

    e. He seems to have only a worldly side, with no spirituality at all.

Are we guilty of being so caught up in the world that we "forget" about spiritual things? Do we think about the "here and now" rather than the future?

2. Jacob was born after Esau, if only by a few minutes, so is the younger son.

3. The promise of the elder serving the younger. (Genesis 25:23)

4. Was Rebekah's favorite son.

   a. A quiet man. (Genesis 25:27)

   b. Stayed among the tents. (Genesis 25:27)

5. Bought Esau's birthright with a bowl of soup.

6. Tricked his father into giving him the blessing, when **he** (Isaac) wanted to give it to Esau.

   a. Rebekah had a hand in the deception.

   b. Tried to act like Esau—Being hairy with the skin of goats.

   c. Has an answer "The Lord *YOUR* God gave me success."

Are we guilty of trying to deceive others, including God by our actions? Do we try to act like something or someone we are not, in order to be more spiritual?

7. Rebekah tells him of Esau's threat of revenge and suggests that he leave.

8. Given Isaac's blessing and "commanded" him to marry someone from his mother's household. (Genesis 28:1-5)

9. Jacob is given the blessing of Abraham.

Jacob comes to Bethel (House of God)

   1. He is tired, and sleeps, using a stone for a pillow.

   2. Has a dream of angels going up and down a ladder.

   3. God confirms the *COVENANT* to him.

      a. Jacobs's children will be numerous.

      b. He anoints the stone and sets it up as an altar. It

will play an important role in his life.

    c.   Jacob promises to give a tithe. (Genesis 28:20-22)

    d.   Takes a vow-- If God will do this, then I will do that.

Jacob arrives at his uncle's house and falls in love with Rachel. (Genesis 29:10-12)

He agrees to work for 7 years to marry her.

God has a law of reaping what you sow.

1.   Now we begin to see the law of reaping and sowing.

    a.   He is tricked into marrying Leah.

    b.   Has to work an additional 7 years.

    c.   Leah has children, (because she is not loved) while Rachel is barren.

    d.   *Laban is blessed because of Jacob.* We see this in scripture where an unbeliever is blessed because of a believer.

    e.   After Joseph is born, Jacob wants to go back to Canaan, but his uncle does not want him to go. Jacob increases his own herds with the help of God.

2. Jacob hears from God again, and leaves Paddan Aram and heads to Canaan.

    a.   Rachel steals the household gods of Laban. These could have been fertility gods.

    b.   He is pursued and caught.

    c.   Laban has a visit from God. Told not to do or say anything bad to Jacob. (Genesis 31:29)

    d.   Jacob had served Laban for 20 years.

    e.   Jacob now has 11 sons and 1 daughter.

Jacob meets with Esau—a happy reunion.

Prior to the reunion, he wrestles with God. He could not overpower Him and *is made lame.* God changes his name to *Israel.*

Jacob insists on a blessing.

Israel means "a prince of God"

In Jacob, the flesh was conquered, not removed, he was made to lean on the Lord. Do we lean on the Lord, or on our own flesh? Do we conquer our bodies, or does the Lord have control?

In Hebrews, Jacob "Worshiped leaning on his staff"

Jacob returns to Bethel—it is to be a spiritual encounter, very much like that at Sinai. The people are told to:

1. Get rid of foreign gods.

2. Purify yourselves.

3. Change your clothes.

4. They build an altar, and worship.

Jacob lived in tents, like Abraham, and Isaac. Looking for a city.

He was concerned about being a witness to those around. (Genesis 34:30)

Are we concerned that we are being a witness to those around us? Are we concerned about the reaction that others have to us?

Rachel dies in Childbirth and is buried at Bethlehem.

Jacob now has 12 sons, and 1 daughter.

1. Reuben

2. Simeon

3. Levi

4. Judah

5. Issachar

6. Zebulun

7. Dan

8. Naphtali
9. Gad
10. Asher
11. Joseph
12. Benjamin
13. Dinah

Isaac dies, and is buried in Hebron, next to Abraham, Sarah, and Rebekah.

Esau and Jacob bury him. God restores relationships.

Jacob is then devastated by the loss of Joseph.

Family suffers during the famine, along with everyone else, and he still trusts God to provide.

What about Christians and suffering?

Jacob sends them to Egypt to get provisions so the family will live. He does not want to send Benjamin—why—because he is all that is left of his beloved Rachel.

Israel now moves to Egypt, at the invitation of Pharaoh, and they settle in the area of Goshen.

Jacob had some misgivings about going to Egypt, but God came and gave him comfort. Told him that he would: (Genesis 46:3-4)

1. Become a great nation.
2. God would go down with them.
3. God would bring them back to Canaan.
4. Joseph would close his eyes.
5. 70 people go to Egypt.

Jacob is 130 years old when they go to Egypt. (Genesis 47:9)

Jacob is greatly honored in Egypt.

1. By Pharaoh—He has Jacob bless him. (Genesis

117

    47:7 and 47:10)

2. Given a very good place to live, the land of Goshen.

3. The Egyptians mourn him for 70 days when he dies.

Jacob lives in Egypt for 17 years. (Genesis 47:28)

He makes Joseph swear to bury him in Hebron.

He then later blesses Joseph's sons, giving the greater blessing to the younger rather than the older.

Jacob blesses all of his sons, with prophetic blessings.

Jacob dies and is buried in Hebron with the others.

Jacob is 147 years old when he dies.

JOSEPH—A FAITH THAT SUSTAINED HIM.

Genesis 37-50, Hebrews 11:21-22.

Name means "may the Lord add" or "adding"

Joseph is the first child of Rachel and Jacob.

Born in Haran before the family returned to Canaan.

He is Jacob's favorite.

1. Given the coat of many colors.

2. Born to him in old age.

He is a shepherd, and also a "spy" or so in the eyes of his brothers. (Genesis 37:2)

Joseph also was a dreamer, with the gift of interpretation and understanding dreams.

His brothers hated him and were jealous toward him.

He is 17 when this occurs. (Genesis 37:2)

1. They would not speak a kind word to him. (Genesis 37:4)

2. They want to kill him. (Genesis 37:19)

   a. 9 of the brothers want to do this,

   b. Reuben wanted to rescue him from them.

      i. To return him to Jacob.

3. Sell Joseph to the Ishmaelites.

   a. To be sold into slavery.

   b. For 20 shekels of silver.

    c.   Taken to Egypt.

  4.   Take the coat, and make it look like killed by a wild animal.

    a.   Jacob tears his clothes.

    b.   Puts on sackcloth.

    c.   Mourns his son many days.

    d.   Refuses to be comforted.

    e.   Jacob weeps for Joseph.

Joseph in Egypt.

  1.   Sold as a slave by the Ishmaelites, who were related. They are second cousins.

    a.   Purchased by Potiphar, captain of the guard for Pharaoh.

    b.   *THE LORD WAS WITH JOSEPH*

    c.   He lived in the house with his master.

    d.   Potiphar realizes that God is blessing him, and so puts him over the entire household.

Are we living such that others can see God in our lives, and are we blessing others?

    a.   Joseph is very well built and handsome.

       i.   Potiphar's wife seduces him.

      ii.   This happens every day. (Genesis 39:10)

Are we able to withstand the sometimes-endless temptations and constant barrage from the enemy like Joseph did?

     iii.   Joseph is falsely accused of rape.

     iv.   Placed into prison.

  2.   Joseph is in prison in Egypt.

    a.   Falsely imprisoned.

    b.   *THE LORD WAS WITH HIM.* (Genesis 39:21)

    c.   God shows him kindness.

    d.   Gives him favor with the prison warden.

    e.   Joseph is put in charge of all the prisoners.

    f.   Joseph is given success in whatever he did. (Genesis 39:23)

    g.   The cupbearer and the baker.

        i.   They have dreams.

        ii.   Joseph interprets the dreams.

        iii.   They happen just as he said.

        iv.   Joseph asked the cupbearer to remember him.

1.   To show him kindness.

2.   To mention him to Pharaoh.

3.   To get him out of prison.

        v.   The cupbearer forgets Joseph.

    h.   *Two* years pass with Joseph in prison.

Are we willing to wait on God? Joseph learned patience and continued to work while he waited. We also must do the same.

    1.   Joseph is released and brought to Pharaoh.

        i.   Pharaoh's dream.

            i.   No one is able to interpret them.

            ii.   Cupbearer remembers Joseph.

    j.   Joseph is sent for.

        i.   First, he shaves.

        ii.   Then he changes his clothes.

    k.   Joseph gives the glory to God.

    l.   Joseph gives the interpretation of the dream.

    m.   Joseph gives advice about what to do.

2. Joseph is placed in a position of honor, second only to Pharaoh. (I wonder if Potiphar is in the room. Does Joseph seek revenge? I do not think so.)

   - Pharaoh places Joseph over the food-gathering project, which includes building storage cities, buying grain, etc. In fact, it says that "without your word, no one will lift hand or foot" (Genesis 41:44)

     a. Joseph is 30 years old when this happens.

     b. He is given a wife and has two sons.

        i. His wife is the daughter of a priest of a false god.

        ii. The sons are born during the first 7 years.

        iii. Jacob later blesses these.

        iv. Manasseh— "God has made me to forget my trouble and my father's household."

           1. Ephraim— "God has made me fruitful in the land of my suffering."

   - All of the people go to Joseph for help during the famine. (Genesis 41:55)

     a. Egyptians come for food

     b. People from other countries come for food.

     c. Joseph's brothers come to get food.

   - Joseph recognized his brothers, but they do not recognize him. At least 22 years had passed since they last saw each other.

     a. The dream is fulfilled.

    b. Only 10 brothers are there the first time.

    c. Joseph is concerned about Benjamin.

    d. Brothers return a second time, and this time with Benjamin.

- Joseph reveals himself to the brothers.

    a. They are worried about revenge.

    b. Joseph does not want revenge, but is able to see the bigger picture, that God sent him ahead to preserve the race.

    c. Genesis 45:5-13.

3. Joseph invites the rest of the family to come to Egypt.

    a. Still 5 years of famine left.

    b. Sent along provisions and carts for the wives and young ones to ride in.

    c. They are to be given the best of the land, the "Land of Goshen" to live in.

    d. Jacob is visited by God and told to go to Egypt.

    e. More than 70 people go down.

    f. They obtain property there and are fruitful and increase in number.

4. Joseph and the rest of the family bury Jacob in Hebron.

5. They return to Egypt, and continue to live, even though the famine is over. *"Life is good in Egypt"*.

    a. Brothers are concerned that Joseph will be after revenge now that Jacob is gone.

    b. Genesis 50:19-21.

6. Joseph lives in Egypt for 93 years, and when he is about to die, he gives instructions to his brothers.

a. Joseph reminds Israel of the land and inheritance promised to them.

b. "God will come and rescue you out of this place" (Genesis 50:24, Hebrews 11:22)—do you think they thought they needed rescuing? Yet God had told Abraham that they would be slaves for 400 years in Egypt.

c. "You must take my bones with you" (Genesis 50:25, Hebrews 11:22)—Why couldn't they have taken him to Canaan at this time??? Yet he was embalmed and placed in a coffin in Egypt.

7. Joseph's bones are taken (Exodus 13:19) and buried in Shechem (Joshua 24:32).

Lessons we can learn:

1. God speaks to us, sometimes in dreams and visions.

2. God has a purpose for our lives.

3. God will bless us, and others because of us.

4. God will use adverse situations to bring glory to Himself.

5. Vengeance belongs to God, not us.

6. Humility and our relationship with God will take us far in His work.

MOSES—A LIFE OF FAITH.

Story of Moses is in Exodus, Numbers, Deuteronomy, Acts 7:22-46, Hebrews 11:23-29.

Moses's story can be broken down into three periods of 40 years each.

Do not know what his Hebrew name was, only his Egyptian name.

Name means "to draw out" or "extraction"

The years in Egypt.

A. Moses is born to Amram and Jochebed, who are slaves in Egypt, from the tribe of Levi.

    1. Moses has two older siblings.

        a. Miriam—His older sister

        b. Aaron—brother who was three years older than him.

    2. His parents hid him for three months from the Pharaoh. (Hebrews 11:23)

        a. Sons were to be thrown into the river girls were to live.

        b. Unable to hide him any longer.

            i. Made a basket out of bulrushes (papyrus).

            ii. Put pitch into it so it would float.

            iii. She set it adrift on the river, releasing the child to God.

        c. Miriam watched and followed on the bank.

3. Pharaoh's daughter finds Moses.

    a. She felt sorry for him.

    b. She knew he was a Hebrew baby.

    c. Miriam offers to get a nurse for him.

    d. Jochebed is hired to nurse Moses.

    e. When he is older, is taken to Pharaoh's daughter, and is then named MOSES. *HE WAS FROM 2 TO 5 YRS OLD.*

B. Moses is raised in the Palace of Pharaoh.

    1. Moses was educated in Egypt. (Acts 7:22)

        a. Wisdom of Egypt.

            i. Science

            ii. Religion

            iii. Philosophy

            iv. Government

        b. Powerful in speech. (Acts 7:22)

        c. Powerful in Action. (Acts 7:22)

        d. Arts and Glory of Egypt.

        e. Life of Court and ceremony.

    2. Moses still knew that he was a HEBREW.

        a. "When he was grown"

            i. He refused to be known as the son of Pharaoh's daughter.

            ii. He chose to be mistreated along with the people.

            iii. He regarded disgrace for Christ rather than treasure of Egypt. (Hebrews 11:25)

        b. Moses knew that he was called to deliver the people.

  i. Thought that if he helped them, they would accept him.

  ii. He killed an Egyptian beating a Hebrew.

  iii. He expected to be accepted.

    1. Was asked "Who made you ruler"

    2. "Who made you a judge over us?"

 c. Moses tried to deliver them by his own strength, and he failed.

 d. Moses was forced to flee for his life.

THE YEARS IS THE DESERT.

A. Moses in Midian.

1. Rescues the daughters of Reuel. (Aka Jethro)

    a. Had 7 daughters.

    b. His name means "Friend of God"

    c. Moses marries Zipporah.

    d. Two sons are born.

        i. One named Gershom (an alien in a foreign land).

        ii. And one named Eliezer (My God is my helper).

2. He is a shepherd for his father-in-law.

3. He is in Midian for 40 years.

    a. A time of refining.

        i. Taking the skills from Egypt and applying them to nomadic life.

        ii. Learning the life of a nomadic shepherd.

    b. A time of religious refreshing.

        i. Spending time with Jethro's family.

        ii. Learning the stories (Genesis?)

        iii. Learning to hear God.

Do we sometimes need to go to the desert in order to "hear God?" Why is this so hard, that we have to go somewhere, is it because we are so busy, we cannot hear God above the noise?

Moses encounters God.

1. The burning bush.

    a. God is in the bush yet does not speak.

    b. Moses "turned aside to see" the bush.

        i. Moses had to choose to see the bush.

        ii. He was willing to turn from the routine to find God.

Do we get so busy, that God puts opportunities in our paths, and we do not "turn aside"?

2. God speaks.

    a. Calls Moses by name.

    b. Warns Moses about His Holiness.

    c. Identifies Himself.

3. Moses obeys.

    a. He answers God.

    b. He hides his face.

    c. He removes his sandals.

4. God calls Moses to the task.

    a. God calls us to a task as well.

    b. God had equipped Moses with his past.

    c. God uses our past to make us what He wants us to be.

5. Moses tries to make excuses.

    a. God listens to the excuses.

    b. God answers and provides the means to overcome them.

We do this, and God does the same thing.

6. Aaron comes to get Moses, and they start on the mission together.

THE FINAL 40 YEARS.

A. Moses in Egypt (part 2)

    1.   Moses and Aaron before the Elders. (Exodus 4:29-31)

        a.   They hear from Aaron.

        b.   They see the signs from Moses.

        c.   They believe.

        d.   *They Worship.*

    2.   They go to Pharaoh.

        a.   He refuses to let them go.

        b.   He makes their lives more difficult.

    3.   The plagues on the Egyptians

        a.   It is a battle of God against the gods of Egypt. (Exodus 12:12)

        b.   It is a showing of the power of God. (Exodus 9:16-17)

        c.   The final plague is the death of the first-born.

            i.   Passover is instituted here.

           ii.   A lesson for future generations. (Still going on today).

          iii.   *God provides a way of escape.*

          iv.   *Christ is our Passover*

    4.   Pharaoh orders them to leave, and asks Moses to "bless him" (Exodus 12:32)

        a.   Moses is as a god to the Egyptians.

        b.   The Egyptians give wealth to the Israelites.

5. Moses leads the people to the Red Sea.

6. The Red Sea parts, due to faith of Moses

    a. People cross over due to their own faith. (Hebrews 11:29)

    b. Cross over on dry ground.

    c. The Egyptians are drowned.

7. Moses leads the people to Mt Horeb, (The mountain of God.)

    a. Receives the Law.

    b. Receives the plan for the Tabernacle.

    c. Moses sees the Glory of God.

8. Moses and the People.

    a. He intercedes for the people.

    b. He leads the people.

    c. He judges the people.

    d. He encourages the people.

    e. He pleads for the people.

    f. He rebukes the people.

9. Moses and God.

    a. Talked to God face to face.

    b. Pleaded with God for the people.

    c. Had to wear a veil because his face glowed.

    d. He had a relationship.

10. Moses unable to lead the people into "Promised Land" because of disobedience.

11. He is able to see it from Mt. Nebo.

12. Moses dies at 120 years old. His eyes were not weak, nor his strength gone.

13. God buries Moses.

14. Satan contends for the body of Moses. (Jude 9)

15. Moses does get into Promised Land at Mt. of Transfiguration.

FAITH OF A NATION.

Hebrews 11:29-30

"By faith they passed through the Red Sea as by dry land, which the Egyptians assaying to do, were drowned."
Hebrews 11:29

Exodus 14:21-30

    A. God delivers the people from their enemies.

    B. They cross on dry ground.

    C. Egyptians are drowned.

Lack of faith—the spies, and the people have to spend 40 years in the wilderness, until that generation dies off. Only two people are allowed to go in that are "fighting age" (20 years or more) Numbers 1:2-3.

    A. Out of Egypt 2 years when the census is taken Joshua and Caleb are among those numbered.

    B. They are probably in their early 20's.

    C. People rebel and are forced to travel until all of them die. Even now, God continues to take care of them.

    D. God requires a second censes in Numbers 26:65. Only Joshua and Caleb are in both censuses.

"By faith the walls of Jericho fell down, after they were compassed about seven days." Hebrews 11:30

Joshua 6:1-24

    A. Jericho is a well-fortified city.

B. Men of war are to march around it once each day, for six days.

C. Men were obedient to Joshua and God.

a. Marched around the city.

b. They did not say a word until ordered to.

D. On the seventh day, they marched around the city seven times, and when the command was given, they shouted.

E. There is no way that they could take the credit for this battle, it had to be from God.

Are we willing followers of the leaders that God has placed over us? Can you see the difference in the two groups of Israelites, the first ones from Egypt, and the next generation?

A FAITH OF WONDERS

Rahab, the harlot.

Hebrews 11:31, Joshua 2:1-24, 6:24-25.

Faith is more than a belief----- it is an action.

A. For 40 years the people of Canaan have been hearing about the Hebrews.

    a. God parting the Red Sea.

    b. Destruction of Sihon and Og.

    c. God's provision in the desert.

B. This had resulted in the people's hearts melting in fear.

C. Everyone's courage had left because of the stories.

D. Rahab makes a statement about God. It could show belief, but it goes much deeper.

    a. The King of Jericho heard and believed the stories but did not come to the same conclusion.

    b. No one else in town has come to the idea that there might be MERCY in the God of the Hebrews. They are trusting in their gods, and in their protective city walls.

    c. Rahab delivers the spies from the guards and tells them to wait so long before returning to Joshua.

    d. She hid them on her roof.

    e. She then asked for mercy for her household.

      f.   She also had to keep the cord in the window.

           i.   The cord was something that she had already.

          ii.   It was a tangible thing that could be felt.

        iii.   This demonstrated her faith.

      g.   She acknowledges that God is the God of heaven and earth.

E.   Three strikes --you're in.

      a.   She was an Amorite, living in Jericho.

      b.   She was a woman.

      c.   She was a prostitute.

Yet with these "strikes" she knew that she had to accept the God of Israel in order to live. She had to accept Him completely, not just a belief.

F.   Because of her actions, she and her household are saved and "saved alive."

G.   She is in the lineage of Jesus. (Matthew 1:5)

Could others have been saved? "Others believed the facts, but they did not believe in God. They never trusted the living God." Was God giving them chances to be saved?

FAITH OF THE JUDGES

During the time of the Judges, God would use the neighboring people to punish the Israelites, and when they would cry out to God, He would send them a Judge to deliver them. They would be okay until the death of the judge, and then they would forget God.

GIDEON—A mighty man of valor.

Story in Judges 6-8

The people have been slaves of the Midians for 7 years, when they begin to cry to God.

    A. Tribes from the south, who had tamed camels.

    B. They would form alliances with others, and then attack.

    C. Would come at harvest, and steal all of the harvest.

    D. "Like locust" Judges 6:5—very numerous.

God sends them a prophet, who reminds them of the past. Judges 6:8-10.

Gideon

    A. Father's name is Joash.

    B. From tribe of Manasseh.

    C. He is the youngest in his family.

    D. Family has an alter to BAAL.

    E. He has 70 sons.

    F. He is threshing wheat in a wine press.

      a.   Why? To keep it from the Midians.

      b.   Very difficult to do.

G.   God appears to him.

      a.   Addresses him as a "mighty man of valor" or "mighty warrior"

      b.   Gideon is startled.

      c.   He questions God- If God is for us, what has happened?

      d.   God tells him to go in his own strength and save Israel. Judges 6:14.

      e.   Gideon explains that he can't do it, and then God tells him He will be with him.

H.   Gideon wants to make sure, so fixes dinner for God.

      a.   He brings it to the place.

      b.   It is burned up as an offering to God.

      c.   Gideon is terrified and thinks he should die.

      d.   Is reassured by God and builds an alter and calls it "The Lord of Peace."

I.   The first job of Gideon.

      a.   Take a bull from your fathers heard. Judges 6:25.

      b.   Tear down the alter of Baal.

      c.   Cut down the grove (Asherah pole)

      d.   Build a proper alter to the Lord your God.

      e.   Make a burnt offering to God using the pole for wood.

      f.   This Gideon did, *at night because he feared the people.* Judges 6:27.

J. The Israelites are furious because their alter is torn down.

    a. How far they have gone from God.

    b. They want Gideon killed. Judges 6:30.

    c. His father's response is great. "If Baal really is a god, he can defend himself when someone breaks down his alter" or "If Baal can't defend himself, what kind of a god is he?"

K. The call to arms.

    a. Gideon sounds the trumpet after the *Spirit of the Lord* comes upon him.

    b. He calls all Manasseh, Asher, Naphtali, and Zebulun.

L. Gideon's Fleece

    a. A test of God?

    b. A test of Faith?

    c. Just to be sure?

M. Too many men.

    a. 32,000 to start with.

    b. God will not share his glory with anyone.

    c. Send them home if afraid. 22,000 men leave.

    d. Still too many—drinking contest. 9,700 men leave.

    e. Now have *only 300 men*

    f. These are the ones that God wants. They are given provisions and a trumpet. MAKES YOU WONDER WHAT IS GOING THROUGH THEIR MINDS?

N. God sends him to be encouraged. Judges 7:9-14

O. Gideon's Response---HE WORSHIPS GOD!

P. The strategy and the plan.

    a. Divides the people into three companies.

    b. Each is given a trumpet, a jar, and a torch.

    c. Blow the trumpets.

    d. Break the jars.

    e. Shout "For the Lord and for Gideon." Judges 7:18

    f. The Lord caused them to turn on each other and kill one another in the camp.

    g. The army continues to chase them and kill them.

    h. Gideon kills the kings. Judges 8:20-21

Q. They ask Gideon to rule over them.

    a. His response— "I will not, nor my son, but THE LORD WILL RULE OVER YOU." Judges 8:22-23

R. Gideon's request.

    a. He asks for the earrings from the *enemies who were Ishmaelite.* He makes an ephod from it, and it becomes an idol to the Israelites, and to the house of Gideon.

S. Gideon dies, and is buried

Gideon is no sooner dead, and the Israelites are again worshiping other gods.

SAMSON FAITH THAT DESERVED A SECOND CHANCE

Story of Samson

Judges 13:1-16:31

The birth of Samson

A. From the tribe of Dan.

B. His mother is barren.

C. Father's name is Manoah

D. An angel of the Lord appears and tells her that she is going to have a son.

    a. She is not to eat anything from Grapes.

    b. She is not to eat anything unclean.

    c. Samson was to be a NAZARITE from his birth until his death.

    d. He would BEGIN to deliver the people from the Philistines. (Judges 13:3-5) This would continue until David.

E. She goes and tells her husband.

    a. HE PRAYS AND ASKS FOR GUIDANCE FROM GOD.

    b. Asks that the angel would come back.

    c. Manoah is a man of faith— "*when* your words

are fulfilled" (Judges 13: 12)

d. He thought it was a man and did not know it was an angel. (V.16)

e. Angel tells him to prepare a burnt offering for the Lord.

f. When the burnt offering is offered, the angel ascended in the flame.

    i. Manoah and wife fall to ground face down.

    ii. Realize that it was an angel.

    iii. He expects to die.

    iv. His wife says "If the Lord had meant to kill us, he would not have accepted the burnt offering, nor showed us these things, nor told us about the birth of our son."

F. A son is born, and he is called Samson. (Judges 13:24)

a. He is a NAZARITE. (Numbers 6:1-21)

    i. Abstain from wine.

    ii. Not eat anything from grapes.

    iii. Not cut his hair.

    iv. Must not go near a dead body.

    v. Stay away from things that are unclean.

b. He wants to marry a Philistine Woman.

    i. His parents ask him why. (Judges 14:3)

    ii. It was God working to get Samson in a position to confront the Philistines.

c. He kills a lion on the way to his wedding.

d. Uses it as an opportunity to ask a riddle of the

guests.

      i. He went aside to a dead animal, which is an unclean animal.

      ii. This was at the Vineyards of Timnah.

      iii. Samson kills 30 philistines to pay off his "Riddle" (Judges 14:19)

   e. His wife is given to his best man. (Judges 14:20)

   f. Samson goes to see his wife but is refused. He destroys their crops.

i. As a result of this, his wife and father-in-law are killed.

ii. Samson then kills many of them.

   g. Samson kills 1,000 men with a jawbone.

      i. Look at his arrogance in Verse 18-19.

SAMSON JUDGES ISRAEL FOR 20 YEARS!

Samson now begins to play games.

A. The prostitute from Gaza. Judges 16:1-3

B. Delilah

    a. He loved her

    b. She was used by the Philistines to get him.

        i. Offered 1100 shekels of silver from each of the leaders.

    c. Samson then plays games with her.

        i. "7 fresh thongs"

        ii. "Ties me with new ropes"

        iii. "Weave my hair on the loom"

        iv. She continued to "NAG" him every day, until. . .

        v. "I have never had my hair cut"

            1. 7 locks or braids of hair

            2. He is made helpless

            3. They take him and gouge out his eyes

            4. Take him to Gaza.

            5. Bind him with bronze chains.

            6. Make him grind in prison.

            7. *HIS HAIR GROWS BACK!*

C. Samson's death

    a. A feast to Dagon, the god of the Philistines.

    b. Bring out Samson to entertain them.

    c. Samson prays for strength to avenge himself for his two eyes.

    d. "Let me die with the Philistines" Judges 16:30.

    e. About 3,000 die with Samson.

    f. He is buried in the tomb of his father.

Lessons to learn from SAMSON

    1. Vows made to God are to be taken seriously. Even though Samson did not voluntarily make the vow, it was still binding.

    2. When Samson did a great deed, it was because the "Spirit of the Lord" came upon him.

    3. God is a God of forgiveness and of second chances.

A FAITH THAT LASTED A LIFETIME

Samuel

Story of Samuel is in I Samuel 1-10, 16, 19, and 25

His name means, "asked of God" or "appointed by God."
His birth and early life.

A. His birth.

      a.   His father was a *Levite*, named ELKANAH

      b.   His mother's name was Hannah.

            i.   She was barren, and asked God for a child.

            ii.   She was the second wife of Elkanah, and he loved her more than his other wife.

            iii.   She was a very devout woman, who trusted God.

            iv.   *She had vowed that her son would be dedicated to God his entire life. HE IS A NAZARITE!*

      c.   He is born into a family that has other siblings from another wife.

B. His early life.

      a.   He is born, and until he is weaned, his mother raises him.

      b.   When he is weaned, (which could be up to age

three) Samuel is taken to the tabernacle, which is at Shiloh and is given to Eli, the priest.

c. The Word of the Lord was very rare at this time. God was not communicating with His people on a regular basis.

d. Eli has a very bad family, and even with this upbringing, *Samuel is to hear from the Lord.* (I Samuel 2:12-17)

e. God calls Samuel. (I Samuel 3:1-18)

    i. Samuel is ministering before the LORD.

    ii. Samuel grows in favor with God and Men. (I Samuel 2:26, Luke 2:52)

    iii. Samuel is called three times and goes to Eli.

    iv. The fourth time he recognizes it is the Lord.

    v. God's message to Samuel.

        1. Destruction of the House of Eli.

C. Samuel continues in the Lord. (I Samuel 3:19-21)

a. All Israel recognizes that he is a prophet.

b. God continues to reveal himself to Samuel.

c. His word spreads to all the country.

D. Samuel the prophet.

a. Tells Eli what is to happen.

b. Samuel is the first to hold the office of a prophet

c. He started a school for prophets, which continued in Israel for a long time.

E. Samuel the intercessor.

a. He led the people in repentance. I Samuel 7:3-4

b. He prayed for the people. V.5

      c.   He prayed again in I Samuel 12:19

F. Samuel the Priest.

      a.   He was a Levite by birth, and God gave him the duties of a Priest.

      b.   He offered Sacrifice. I Samuel 7:9-10.

      c.   He prayed for the people. I Samuel 7:9.

      d.   He anointed the kings. I Samuel 10:1, 16:13.

      e.   He built an alter to the Lord at Ramah.

G. Samuel the Judge.

      a.   Samuel is the last of the Judges.

      b.   He judges the people all of his live. I Samuel 7:15.

      c.   He had a regular circuit that he took to judge them. V 16.

      d.   He was also a military leader. I Samuel 7:2-13.

H. He was a man of courage.

      a.   Confronted Saul about his sin, and killed AGAG, king of the Amalekites.

      b.   He anointed David as King of Israel.

I. Samuel was a man of deep conviction and feelings.

      a.   He felt that he was being rejected when Israel wanted a king. I Samuel 8:7.

      b.   He had sons who did not follow in his footsteps.

      c.   What do you do when you raise a child right, and they go wrong?

      d.   Samuel mourns over Saul, and God has to tell him to stop, and to go anoint David to be king   I Samuel 15:36-16:1

J. Samuel dies. I Samuel 25:1

      a.   He is mourned by all Israel.

      b.   He is buried in Ramah.

J.   A witch for Saul brings him up from the grave. I Samuel 28:11-20.

      a.   It was Samuel.

      b.   He prophesied about the death and defeat of Saul.

      c.   He told that the kingdom would be given over to David.

Lessons from Samuel.

1.   The importance of a vow.

2.   The importance of training up a child.

3.   The impact we can have on others due to our lives being lived for the Lord.

4.   God has a job for each of us to do if we will only be willing vessels.

FAITH OF A KING

**David—Story is in I Samuel 16-31, II Samuel,
I Chronicles 15, 25, and I Kings 1+2.**

Name means "well beloved"

A. Early life of David.

    a. Born in Bethlehem.

    b. Youngest of Jesse's 8 sons.

    c. The Shepherd of Jesse's flock.

        i. Had defeated a lion.

        ii. Had defeated a bear.

    d. Wrote psalms while took care of sheep.

    e. Anointed as King of Israel.

    f. Killed Goliath.

    g. Hired to play for King Saul to sooth his evil moods.

B. David's life before being king.

    a. Leader of the armies of Saul.

    b. Distinguished himself as a man of war. "Saul has killed his thousands, and David his ten thousands."

    c. Became Saul's son-in-law.

    d. Befriends Jonathan, Saul's son.

    e. Eats at the table of Saul.

    f. Forced to flee from Saul and continues for a long time.

    g. Gathers a group of soldiers, and they keep running from Saul.

      h.   Joins with the Philistines for a while.

      i.   Does not harm Saul, even though the chance presents itself.

      j.   Mourns over the death of Saul and Jonathan.

C.   David as King.

      a.   King in Hebron over Judah and Benjamin. (7 years)

      b.   David is anointed over all the tribes and moves the capital to Jerusalem.

      c.   The Davidic covenant. II Samuel 7:4-16.

            i. 1st a covenant to the race---Adam.

            ii. 2nd a covenant to a nation—Abraham.

            iii. 3rd a covenant to a tribe—Judah.

            iv. 4th a covenant to a family—David.

      d.   David's sin(s).

            i.   Numbering the people.

                1.   A plague upon the land.

                2.   Seeing an angel of the Lord.

                3.   Purchasing the place that was to become the Temple.

            ii.   Taking Bathsheba.

                1.   Her becoming pregnant.

                2.   Covering up the affair.

            iii. Having Uriah killed.

                1.   Consequences of this:

                    a.   David repents.

                    b.   Child dies.

                    c.   Trouble in David's house from then on.

e. David's troubles.

    i. His daughter is raped by her half-brother.

    ii. His son—Amnon is killed by his half-brother, Absalom.

    iii. Absalom's rebellion—all that Nathan said would come to pass does.

        1. David's concubines are raped in plain view of everyone.

        2. David forced to flee the capital.

        3. Joab kills Absalom.

f. David selects Solomon as his successor.

    i. He charges Solomon with building the temple.

    ii. He has Solomon swear to get revenge on people who have done him wrong.

g. David dies.

h. He is buried in Jerusalem, after ruling for 40 years.

Lessons we can learn from David.

A. Even though he messed up, he was repentant.

B. God will sometimes call a person, but they have to wait for God's timing.

C. David was very patient.

D. He was a "man after God's own heart.

LEVEL 6

Seeker of Servanthood

The disciple is not above his master,
Nor the servant above his lord.
Matthew 10:24

If any man serve me, let him follow me;
And where I am, there shall also my servant be:
If any man serve me, him will my Father honor.
John 12:26

By love serve one another.
Galatians 5:13

JESUS, OUR FOCUS

A. Focus—keeping an item in view

    a. Keeping it "clearly" in view

        i. If it gets fuzzy, then it is not in focus

        ii. Need to keep Jesus *CLEARLY* in view, not allow Him to get fuzzy

        iii. Hebrews 12:1-2— "let us fix our eyes on Jesus"

            1. If we want God's best for us, we need to start with the lives of those who have gone before—they were able to keep going, and so can we

            2. We need to run a race—keep going. This would entail getting rid of those things that could keep us from being successful

            3. The race must be run with perseverance. We have to keep working. We may not see the end, but we must continue to run to the finish.

            4. Our **focus** has to be Jesus—why? He is the author and finisher of our faith. *We have to continue to have Him as our focus; otherwise, our faith will not become complete.*

    b. We can lose our focus by letting other things become our focus. We can focus on items before or behind what we should be focusing on. We need to keep our focus on only one thing

    i.   Before—the Pharisees would focus on the LAW. They were so focused on the Law, that they could not see Jesus when He came, and fulfilled that Law.

    ii.   After—people can focus on what is ahead—Heaven, which they again lose track of today, and our focus leaves Jesus. When this occurs, it is easy to be led astray by fables, false doctrine, etc. This would result in our becoming ineffective in sharing the Gospel.

c.   So much wants to distract us, and take our focus off of Jesus.

    i.   Matthew 14:22-33—As long as Peter's focus was on Jesus, he was successful. When he took his eyes off of Jesus, He lost his focus and sank.

    ii.   Mark 4:18-19—the cares of the world also can cause us to lose our focus.

B.   Why focus on Jesus?

a.   *JESUS IS OUR LORD*—He is our Lord and Savior. As our Lord, we are to please Him in everything we do. We will know when we are not pleasing to Him if we keep our focus on Him.

b.   *JESUS IS OUR EXAMPLE*—He is *our pattern or example* to follow. I Peter 2:21

c.   *JESUS IS THE HEART OF THE GOSPEL*—the entire Gospel centers on Jesus. Paul speaks of many things and talks about their importance. He says this is of "first importance." I Corinthians 15:3-4. He felt that the most important thing is not deep theology, ideals, or prophecy. He was not telling us to look for the Anti-Christ, or to preach the four-step way to salvation. Rather he says the most important thing is Jesus—His death, burial, and resurrection.

    i.   This is what most cults deny. They say that Jesus was a good man, a great example, a good teacher, a great prophet, etc., but He did not die, or rise from the dead.

    ii.   Paul said in II Timothy 2:7-9 that the Gospel is *Jesus raised from the dead.* That is the entire Gospel.

C. Our very name says that we belong to Christ. If we are Christians, then we need to:

    a.   Know Him—not just knowledge *about* Him, but personally have a relationship with Him as Lord and Savior—some do one but not the other. Our relationship needs to continue to be *alive and growing.*

    b.   Show Him—we will live like He lived. This would include:

        i.   James 1:22—being a doer

        ii.   Matthew 25:31-46—sheep and goats

        iii.   John 21: 15-17—feed my sheep

    c.   Go with Him—follow His commandments, including being a testimony of Jesus.

D. We are Jesus's focus—many times the Bible speaks of Jesus "fixing" His eyes on someone. He would then have compassion for them and heal them. He came to die for US so we can live for Him.

The Bible is God's dealing with us. The Old Testament showed many types and shadows of Christ. Again, the focus of the Old Testament was to bring man into an everlasting relationship (covenant) with God. The relationship became fuzzy as man sinned and tried to "fix" it by turning the relationship into "religion" With Jesus the focus is renewed. It is through Him and only Him that the relationship is put back into place. God took the initiative. We need to accept the Gift and then continue to focus on Jesus.

In every picture, there is a focus, and it is to be the same in our lives. We are to be focused or centered on Jesus. Just as in a wedding, the focus is on the bride, so we as Christians need to have as our focus Jesus. Our goal is to be like Jesus. Every religion in the world has something to focus on. Most deal with works. Judaism focus is on the Law. Catholicism has their focus on the mother, not the Son. Islam deals with following the ideas of Mohammad, which include subjugating the world and converting them by force. We as Christians have someone, and His name is Jesus. It is easy to get out of focus, and even though He is still in the picture, we sometimes lose sight of Jesus when our lives get out of focus. "To be like Jesus, to be like Jesus, all I ask is to be like Him. All through lives journey, from here to glory, all I ask is to be like Him" So goes the old hymn, and so too needs to go our relationship with our Lord. We need to increase in the knowledge of Jesus.

Just as Paul preached only Jesus, and Him crucified, so we need to be more aware of the Jesus we are portraying to others. As John said, "I must decrease, but He must increase." We, as the Bride of Christ, need to keep our focus on the Groom. This is what we are to be waiting for. It is fun to think about philosophy, prophecy, history, all of these different sciences, but we must never forget, or crowd out Jesus, our main focus. He is whom everything in our lives should revolve around. He needs to be at the center of our universe, just as we are the center of His.

HAVING THE MIND OF CHRIST

A. In order to be successful in God's sight we must:

    a. Want to be successful— (want God's best)

    b. *Focus* on Jesus/have a *relationship* with Him

    c. *Make* friends with the Holy Spirit

    d. *Meditate* on God's Word

    e. *Listen* to the voice of God and *obey*

    f. Have the *mind of Christ*

B. I Corinthians 2:16, Philippians 2:5— *"but we have the mind of Christ"*

    a. How can we have the "mind of Christ"?

        i. Our priorities must be the same as His

        ii. *Two* types of priorities

            1. *Eternal*—things that will last forever

            2. *Temporal*—things that will fade away (earthly priorities)

        iii. *Eternal perspectives*—where do these come from and how can we get them?

            1. II Corinthians 4:16-18

                a. "The outward man"—perish TEMPORAL

                b. "The inward man"—renewed day by day ETERNAL

                c. "Light affliction"—short lived (persecution) TEMPO-

RAL

d. "Glory"—ETERNAL

e. "Things which are seen"—things we can tell with our senses (touch, taste, smell, hear, experience)—TEMPORAL

f. "Things which are not seen"—this is FAITH—Hebrews 11:1--ETERNAL

2. II Corinthians 5:7—how we are to be *"FOR WE WALK BY FAITH, NOT BY SIGHT"*

a. If this is true we are to be:

i. *DIRECTED BY ETERNAL*

ii. *GOVERNED BY ETERNAL*

iii. *CONTROLLED BY ETERNAL*

iv. *MOTIVATED BY ETERNAL*

b. In order to be this, we must:

i. *Use God's Word* as a mirror to see what the eternal is

ii. *Allow the Holy Spirit* to make us into the image of Jesus Christ

iii. Be willing to *trust God completely*

c. *JESUS IS THE LORD OF BOTH ETERNAL AND TEMPORAL. HE WILL BLESS US IN BOTH REALMS, BUT ONLY IF WE HAVE OUR PRIORITIES RIGHT*

1. Matthew 6:19-21, I Timothy 6:9-11—do not pursue wealth. Does this mean that God wants you to be des-

titute and poor? I do not think so. I think that this also depends on what our priorities are. To the one who has much, more will be required. (Regarding as to how the wealth is used.) If we pursue wealth, then it *can* become our master (Matthew 6:24) rather than Jesus.

2. Matthew 6:31-33—what are we to pursue (seek or go after)?

   a. Seek the kingdom of God.

   b. Pursue righteousness, godliness, faith, love, patience, and meekness. (I Timothy 6:11)

   c. Philippians 4:8

3. Philippians 4:19—let God do the supplying. He knows what we need and has the provision to provide.

SANCTIFICATION

What does it mean to be sanctified?

1. To be set apart

2. To bring glory to God

3. To have a specific purpose

4. It is an act of both separation from that which is evil and dedication to God.

A. We believe in "progressive sanctification"

    i. We are sanctified at salvation--instantaneously

        1. When we accept Jesus as Lord and Savior, we are declared "clean" and "holy" before God--I Corinthians 6:11 I John 1:7 I Corinthians 1:2

        2. Paul addresses all Christians as "saints"

            a. What is a "saint"

            b. Anyone who believes in Jesus

        3. We are declared dead to sin—Romans 6:1-4, 6-7, 11

    ii. The process of sanctification is a continual process

        1. We now have a choice

            a. We chose each day to serve God or self I Corinthians 15:31, Romans 6:13

            b. We are in a spiritual battle, and we must not excuse ourselves from the moral responsibility that we have in Christ

i. We can blame weakness—but Philippians 4:13

    1. Lack of desire--repentance

2. Lack of striving—discipleship

        ii.Today there is a lack of conviction, and a desire for comfort

1. *Sanctification is a process*

    a. There will be chastening—Hebrews 12:10-11

    b. There will be growth—2 Peter 3:18

    c. There will be work—Philippians 2:12-13

    d. There will be avoiding some things—Romans 6:1-2, 2 Corinthians 7:1 I Peter 1:13-14

2. *Sanctification is being "alive to God"—Romans 6:11*

    a. The Holy Spirit gives us the *POWER* to do this—I Corinthians 6:11, 2 Thessalonians 2:13

    b. It is achieved by *FAITH* Acts 26:18

    c. It is through the *TRUTH of SCRIPTURE*-- John 17:17

    d. It is being *READY FOR JESUS RETURN*—Revelation 19:7

    e. It is *COMMUNION WITH CHRIST* John 15:4

    f. It is *DOCTRINE*—Ephesians 4:11-13

    g. It is *WHOLESOME LIVING*—Philippians 4:8-9

3. What about backsliding—

    a. What is it?

        i. The opposite of sanctification

        ii.A gradual movement away from God that leads to damnation

    b. *Dangerous because—*

        i. Subtle nature of moving away from God

        ii.It causes us to lose our love for Christ—Revelation 2:4

4. The final result –a new potential

    a. Perfection—Matthew 5:48, I John 3:2

THE CHURCH

A. What is it?

    a. The Body of Christ—I Corinthians 12:12-31

        i. Jesus is the head Ephesians 1:22-23

        ii.People

        iii. Individuals

        iv. We need each other, cannot be isolated

        v. Arranged as God sees fit I Corinthians 12:18

        vi. Are to support and strength each other

        vii.   Is living organism

    b. Members of the Church

        i. Accepted Jesus as Lord—Acts 2:47

        ii.Called by names:

            1. Saints—Romans 1:7, Ephesians 1:1

            2. Brethren—Romans 8:29, I Corinthians 1:10

        iii. Collectively:

            1. Bride of Christ 2 Corinthians 11: 2, Ephesians 5:25-27, Revelation 19:7-8

            2. Temple of God I Corinthians 3:16

            3. Body of Christ Romans 12:4-5

B. What is the mission of the Church?

    a. Outward—evangelization Mark 16:15-20 Acts 1:8

        i. To tell others about Christ

        ii.Commanded by Jesus—great commission

        iii. Only with help of Holy Spirit

b.   Inward—edification

        i. Gather for worship

        ii. Teaching

        iii. Prayer for each other

        iv. Hold each other accountable

c.   Upward—worship—we are the priests

        i. Bring glory to God

           1.   Praise

           2.   Singing

           3.   Offering

           4.   Gifts of the spirit

           ii.   Worship in spirit and in truth—John 4:23-24

LEVEL 7

Seeker of Change

Are changed into the same image from glory to glory,
even as by the Spirit of the Lord.
2 Corinthians 3:18

And be not conformed to this world: but be ye
transformed by the renewing of your mind,
that ye may prove what is that good, and acceptable,
and perfect will of God.
Romans 12:2

Finally, brethren, whatsoever things are true,
whatsoever things are honest, whatsoever things are just,
whatsoever things are pure, whatsoever things are lovely,
whatsoever things are of good report, if there be any
virtue, and if there be any praise, think on these things.
Philippians 4:8

LETTING GOD CHOOSE

A. Receiving God's Best

    a. Must want to have God's best

    b. Focus and be connected to Jesus

    c. Meditate on God's Word

    d. Relationship with the Holy Spirit

    e. Hear and obey God's voice

    f. Must have our priorities right

B. *We must let God do the choosing.*

        i. Do we trust God to know what is best for us?

        ii. Luke 12:32—Kingdom

        iii. Matthew 6:31-33—needs

        iv. James 1:17—every good and perfect gift

        v. Luke 11:11-13—gifts and the Holy Spirit

        vi. Philippians 4:11-13—contentment with what God has for US

        vii. II Corinthians 3:4-6—our sufficiency is in God

        viii. Psalm 47:1-9, v.4—God chooses our inheritance

        ix. John 15:14-17—*God has chosen US— why-to go and bring forth fruit*

        x. What God gives us is what HE wants us to have. This is the greatest realization of all. Yeah, we may have to suffer, and go through persecution, but the end result is knowing that HE is there. If we are to become totally destitute and without a dime, He is still there. I can trust Him, and not myself. HE is the one that I am to do all things for. He is my audience and the source of everything I have and am. ‚

　　xi. "God gives His best to those who leave the choice to Him."

b.　We must be willing to do as Jesus Commanded—GO!

　　i. Sharing our faith is not an option, but rather a commandment.

　　　　1.　Acts 1:8

　　　　2.　Matthew 28:18-20

　　ii.　Many different ways to share our faith

　　　　1.　"Without an argument"

　　　　2.　The four spiritual laws

　　　　3.　The A-B-C's of salvation

　　　　4.　Tell what God has done in your life (be a witness for Jesus—give a firsthand account)

　　　　5.　FOLLOW THE HOLY SPIRIT'S LEADING

HOLY VESSELS

God gave the instructions of how to build the Tabernacle to Moses while he was on Mount Sinai. This "blueprint" showed the size, the material, and the furniture of the Tabernacle. There were many different types of vessels for the worship in the Tabernacle.

The Tabernacle was a place set apart for the worship of God. It was the dwelling place of God among the people of Israel. This was the place that God would meet them and that they were to go to for forgiveness of sins. In the New Testament WE are the Tabernacle. We are the dwelling place of the Holy Spirit. Our sins are forgiven with the sacrifice of Jesus on the cross. We are a temple not made by hands. God has placed His Law on our hearts and has given us the Holy Spirit to teach and guide us in how to follow Him. So, what about our part? Do we have to do anything, or do we just coast along?

God has given us a job, and that is to be an order of priests to worship Him. We also are to work at keeping our vessels pure and clean. First we will look at being a priest.

In 1st Peter 2:9 we are called among other things a "Royal Priesthood." What does it mean to be a priest, and what were their duties? How does that apply to us today and how can we be priests to God?

What was the task of a PRIEST? His job is to SERVE THE LORD!

A.   His first priority is to serve God, not himself

> a.   Was not to have an inheritance of the Land
>
> b.   Was not to be drunk

B. Secondly, he is called By God—He is separated from the rest of the people for a special task

    a. Aaron was separated from all the Levites for the task of being the High Priest

    b. The Priest was not to be like others. He is not to mourn for the dead

C. He is appointed for a specific task—to offer the sacrifices for the people. He acts as the intermediary for the people.

    a. He offers the sacrifices

    b. He burns the offering

    c. He prays for the people

    d. He brings the Blood to the Mercy Seat for the Atonement of the People

    e. He had people who helped him, the Levites who were to help with the sacrifices, musicians, burning incense (like Zacharias in Luke 1:8-9), moving the Tabernacle, and teaching the people (like Ezra)

Before the priest could offer for the people, he had to offer for himself, and make himself clean before the Lord. This is what we need to do, we must be:

    A. Consecrated—set apart

    B. Purified—being clean (pure)

    C. Clean—being washed by the Blood of Jesus

In the Old Testament, there was a Hereditary Priesthood, who had to be from the lineage of Aaron--However that changed with the death of Jesus. HE is our High Priest Hebrews 8:1, 9:11-14. What does that do to us? It makes us like the Levites, who were the INHERITANCE OF THE PRIESTLY FAMILY. THEREFORE, WE ARE THE INHERITANCE OF JESUS!

There is only ONE HIGH PRIEST—which is Jesus
What does that make us?

> A. We are a CHOSEN GENERATION
>
> B. We are a ROYAL PRIESTHOOD
>
> C. We are a HOLY NATION
>
> D. We are a PECULIAR PEOPLE

When Aaron was sanctified as a Priest unto God, Moses took the blood of the offering and put some on Aaron's right ear, his right thumb, and his right big toe. I think this is to show the three parts of our work for God, the HEARING, DOING AND GOING:

> 1. Hearing—we are to listen to God. How is this done?
>
>> a. By reading the Scripture—We are to study, to read, to meditate on the Word of God
>>
>> b. By listening—when we pray, we should spend part of that time waiting for a response. God, by the Holy Spirit will speak to us
>>
>> c. By conversation—Listen to what God is telling others. Often, He speaks through preaching, the words of other Christians, and by the confirmation of others.
>>
>> d. By supernatural—God still uses dreams and visions.

As we listen to God, we must weigh everything by the Word of God. Satan wants to twist and confuse us, and it is only as we fill ourselves with the Bible and especially with the words of Jesus that we will be able to come against Satan. Our weapon is the sword of the Spirit, which is the word of God. Ephesians 6:17. If there is a message in tongues, preaching, teaching on the TV, radio, internet, music, or anything else it must match the Bible.

We are told to try the spirits 1st John 4:1. As we continue to get closer to the return of Jesus, Satan will do all he can to deceive the Christians.

2. Doing—we are to do what Jesus tells us to do. How do we know?

   a. Jesus communicates what we are to do in the same way as hearing, but we have a responsibility to act upon it.

   b. We must consider who we are doing what for. What is our motive? Why are we doing what we are doing? I Corinthians 10:31, Colossians 3:17

   c. What if we have a question or concern? God has given us His standard to measure all things against. Philippians 4:8

   d. As with food, if in doubt, throw it out! We must be sure that what we are doing will bring glory and honor to Jesus. We are new in Christ; the old sinful way of life is done, and we must continue in newness of life. 2nd Corinthians 5:17-18

3. Going—we are to go and tell people about Jesus. The great commission is to Go into all the world and preach the good news. We are to be witnesses of all that Jesus has done for us. Some feel that they do not have anything to tell about. If you have been forgiven of your sins that is the greatest thing that anyone can share.

We are not only to have the job of a priest, but we are also called to be Holy Vessels. What is a vessel, and why are we called this?

A vessel is an item that is used for holding something. A vessel can be made out of anything, glass, metal, wood, clay but they all have the same purpose, to hold or contain something.

The first person called a vessel is Saul, who is renamed Paul after Jesus meets him on the road to Damascus. Acts 9:15.

What are we to do as a vessel?

A. First of all, we are to be a vessel that belongs to Jesus. If we have not been saved that is the first and most important thing to do.

B. Second, we must be a willing vessel. We must let Jesus do to us what HE wants to do. Sometimes that would be to be broken. Since we were once a vessel of Satan's then we need to be remade into the image of Christ. Since HE was broken on the cross, so we also need to be broken of our own will and selfishness and pride in order for Jesus to come and fix us. Jeremiah 18:1-7, Romans 9:20-24

C. We must also be vessels that are broken and poured out. We have a treasure, Salvation, which the entire world must have. In order for that treasure to get out, we must be broken and pour out the treasure. 2nd Corinthians 4:7, Mark 14:3-9

D. We must be Holy Vessels. Jesus cannot live in an unholy body. Since He has decided to dwell within us, He makes us Holy at the moment of salvation, and then we have a responsibility to keep ourselves Holy. 1st Thessalonians 4:1-4, Philippians 4:8, 2nd Timothy 2:15 and 22-25

E. We must be vessels that will do whatever Jesus wants us to do. As long as we are doing what Jesus asks us to do, we will be a vessel of Honor. 2nd Timothy 2:20-21

It does not matter if we are the highest honor or the lowest honor, we are in the service of our King, Jesus. As servants of Jesus Christ, we have been called to take the gospel to the entire world. We must not let pride get in the way. It is only as we make ourselves available to Jesus that He can use us. We are victorious and have overcome through Jesus. John 16:33

THE "NEW" CHURCH

Often, we have to relearn the terminology of a concept in order to get it right. This means a change in the "lingo" that we use. Often, a word can have many different definitions, and we need to look at which one is the best for what we are trying to get across. Many of the concepts of "Church" need to be changed from what we often think about.

The first concept that needs to be adjusted is in the meaning of the word.

Some of them are:

1. a building—such as church building
2. an event—like "doing church"
3. a specific place— "I'll meet you at church"
4. an institution—Church of God, Baptist Church

These are hard to break because we have been brainwashed into thinking that this is what church is about. However, Jesus did not have this in mind when He spoke about church. The church that Jesus spoke about is the "Body of Believers." In other words, the church is not a thing, but a person, it is us. We are the Church. Jesus said that HE would build His church, not the disciples. It is only as we yield to HIM that we can let HIM do the work that is needed for the Church to grow.

WE ARE THE BRIDE

Who are we?

1. A royal priesthood
2. A child of the King
3. A chosen generation
4. A new creation
5. Adopted into God's family
6. Beloved of God
7. Bride of Christ

Weddings are a special time today as in the Bible—A Wedding at the time of Christ contained three aspects—1—a betrothal, 2—the bridegroom claiming his bride, 3—marriage supper at the home of the Groom. Our spiritual lives follow this as well. Our Betrothal took place when we accepted Jesus as our Savior. That is in the past. We now are WAITING for the next two parts—the RAPTURE and the MARRIAGE SUPPER. What takes place between the betrothal and the bride groom appearing was for the groom to make the house ready, and the bride to prepare herself. This entailed a lot of WORK.

Who is Jesus? —the Bridegroom

Matthew 9:15, Mark 2:19-20, Luke 5:34-35, John 3:29

What is HE doing—John 14:1-3

We are the BRIDE—Revelation 19:6-9

1. The marriage of the Lamb is come
2. The WIFE has made herself ready

    a. How—by keeping herself pure

185

       i.   Colossians 3:1-17

1. need to put off old
   - a. fornication
   - b. uncleanness
   - c. evil affections
   - d. lust
   - e. covetousness
   - f. idolatry
   - g. anger
   - h. wrath
   - i. malice
   - j. blasphemy
   - k. filthy communication
   - l. lying

2. need to put on new Colossians 3:12-17, II Peter 1:5-8
   - a. knowledge
   - b. mercy
   - c. kindness
   - d. humility
   - e. meekness
   - f. patience
   - g. forgiveness
   - h. love
   - i. peace of God
   - j. thankfulness
   - k. WORD OF GOD

       ii.   Ephesians 4:20-5:21

Level 7 - Seeker of Change

1. put off the old

    a. lying

    b. lust

    c. stealing

    d. bad language

    e. destructive language

    f. bitterness

    g. anger

    h. malice

    i. sexual sin

    j. covetousness

    k. filthiness

    l. whoremonger

    m. unclean person

    n. idolater

    o. foolishness

    p. drunkenness

2. put on the new

    a. truth

    b. renewing you mind

    c. righteousness

    d. holiness

    e. unity

    f. work

    g. charitable/generous

    h. edifying

    i. kind

        j. forgiving

        k. followers of God

        l. love as Christ loved us

        m. thankful

        n. wise

        o. careful

        p. redeeming the time

        q. understanding

        r. filled with the Spirit

3. The WEDDING GARMENT is provided for us Revelation 19:7-8

    a. FINE LINEN

        i. CLEAN

        ii. WHITE

            1. What is it—the RIGHTEOUSNESS OF THE SAINTS

            2. How do we obtain it—THROUGH THE BLOOD OF THE LAMB

4. We are called BLESSED Revelation 19:9

TO THE WHO FIRST?

A. Who are we? —we are CHRISTIANS and that means we are to take the GREAT COMMISSION seriously—THESE ARE THE LAST INSTRUCTIONS THAT CAME FROM OUR COMMANDER.

B. What is the GREAT COMMISSION? —to be witnesses for Christ and to tell others about HIM—We do not do the conversion, but the Holy Spirit is the one who draws us to that Relationship with the Father.

    a. Acts 1:8— "But ye shall receive power, after that the Holy Ghost is come upon you and ye shall be witnesses unto me both in Jerusalem, and in all Judea, and in Samaria, and unto the uttermost part of the earth."

    b. Luke 24:46-49— "And said unto them, 'Thus it is written, and thus it behooved Christ to suffer, and to rise from the dead the third day: 47 And that repentance and remission of sins should be preached in His name among all nations, beginning at Jerusalem. 48 And ye are witnesses of these things. 49 And, behold, I send the promise of my Father upon you: but tarry ye in the city of Jerusalem, until ye be endued with power from on high.'"

    c. Matthew 28:18-20— "And Jesus came and spake unto them saying, "All power is given unto me in heaven and in earth. 19 Go ye therefore and teach all nations, baptizing them in the name

of the Father, and of the Son, and of the Holy
Ghost: 20 Teaching them to observe all things
whatsoever I have commanded you: and, lo, I
am with you always, even unto the end of the
world. Amen."

C. TO THE JEW FIRST

    a. If we are to follow the example of Jesus, Paul,
Peter, and the other disciples, then we are re-
sponsible to take the Gospel first to the Jew.

        i. The JUDGEMENT OF GOD—is going
to be on all

            1. Romans 2:8-11—"But unto them
that are contentious, and do not obey
the truth, but obey unrighteousness,
indignation and wrath, 9 tribulation
and anguish, upon every soul of
man that doeth evil, of the Jew first,
and also of the Gentile; 10 but glory,
honor, and peace, to every man that
worketh good, to the Jew first, and
also to the Gentile: 11 For there is
no respect of persons with God."

        ii. The SALVATION OF GOD—is also for
all

            1. Romans 1:16— "For I am not
ashamed of the gospel of Christ: for
it is the power of God unto salvation
to everyone that believes; to the Jew
first, and also to the Greek"

            2. Romans 10:9-13— "That if thou
shall confess with thy mouth the
Lord Jesus, and shall believe in
thine heart that God has raised Him
from the dead, thou shall be saved.

10 For with the heart man believes unto righteousness; and with the mouth confession is made unto salvation. 11 For the scripture saith, "Whosoever believeth on Him shall not be ashamed. 12 For there is no difference between the Jew and the Greek: for the same Lord over all is rich unto all that call upon Him. 13 For whosoever shall call upon the name of the Lord shall be saved."

b. THE GREAT COMMISSION—IN ROMANS FOLLOWS THIS VERSE.

    i. Romans 10:14-15— "How then shall they call on Him in whom they have not believed? And how shall they believe in Him of whom they have not heard? And how shall they hear without a preacher? 15 And how shall they preach, except they are sent? As it is written, "How beautiful are the feet of them that preach the gospel of peace and bring glad tidings of good things!"

D. Our Lord, Jesus was raised in a Jewish home, by a devout Jewish couple who adhered to the Law.

E. Jesus came as the King of the Jews—yet was not received as the Messiah by the "Religious Leaders"

F. Jesus will return as the King of the Jews—and will rule from Jerusalem

G. Our "Christian Heritage" owes much to the Jews

    a. Communion—from Passover meal

    b. Baptism—from the Mikva that Jews would do to be clean

  c. Old Testament—our source of scripture

H. Why is it hard to reach Jews with the Gospel?

  a. About 95% of Jews are atheist

  b. Many Jews feel they are "in" because they are Jews

  c. Have the Old Testament

  d. Our lack of concern

    i. "Christ Killers"

    ii. History- "Church" abuse of them

      1. Crusades

      2. Inquisition

      3. Anti-Semitism

    iii. TRUE vs. not-true Christian

I. The Jews today are just like the ones at the time of Jesus— looking for a Messiah, one to deliver them

  a. At time of Jesus, wanted a military leader to get rid of oppressors and bring PEACE, and today in Israel want same thing

  b. Jesus came the first time to bring them PEACE—through relationship with God

  c. He will be the military leader and get rid of the oppressors when He returns the second time, as King of the Jews

  J. This second coming is right around the corner. ARE WE READY? Have we done what we are to do, to the JEW first?

MINISTRY OF ALL BELIEVERS

A. Mission of the church

    a. Evangelization of the lost

    b. Edification of the Body of Christ

    c. Worship of God

B. All believers are considered to have a role in the PRIEST-HOOD to God-I Peter 2:9-10, Exodus 19:5-6

    a. This role is to fulfill the three-fold mission of the church

    b. We have all been called to win the lost—Mark 16:15-20 Acts 6:8

        i. What can a believer expect when he or she ministers?

            1. Signs

            2. Wonders

    a. Healing

    b. Demonic encounters

    c. Supernatural protection

        ii. We do not go alone—have the Lord working with us

        iii. This is for all believers—Luke 10:19-20

        iv. Why do we not see these things occurring today?

            1. Our own lack of faith—Matthew 17:17-20

            2. Our own unbelief

3. Could it be our lack of Holiness?

C. God has established leadership roles within the church—Ephesians 4:11-16, I Corinthians 12:27-31

    a. Apostles and Prophets

        i. Apostles—were called by Jesus, given a direct commission from the Lord to perform a specific task

        ii. Prophets—one who conveys God's message to men

            1. Gift of prophecy—I Corinthians 14:3, 22, 29

            2. Can be men or women—Acts 21:8-9

        iii. Evangelists—one who proclaims the Gospel

            1. Jesus's death

            2. Jesus's burial

            3. Jesus's resurrection

            4. Jesus's ascension

            5. Jesus's return

        iv. Pastors

            1. See that spiritual needs of congregation are meet—Acts 20:28

            2. Qualifications for a Pastor—I Timothy 3:2-7, Titus 1:7-9

        v. Teachers

             1. To expound the Word of God for training the people to grow in fellowship and be firmly grounded in the faith

            2. Are answerable for the truth they

        teach

    3. Encourage one another in "stretch-ing"

vi. Deacons Philippians 1:1, I Timothy 3:8-13, Acts 6:3-6

    1. "Ministers" to the people

    2. Responsible for other areas of ministry—so the disciples could continue in prayer and teaching

vii. Putting dinners together

viii. Counting the offering

ix. Maintaining the building

x. Mowing the grass

xi. Etc. etc. etc.

xii. Purpose of the ministry—Ephesians 4:12

    1. Leaders are not to do all of the work, but equip others to find their place in the "BODY" as well

    2. Encourage one another

DIVINE HEALING

A. Sickness and death came about because of the fall of man (sin)

B. Sickness is permitted by God because of sin and disobedience—Exodus 15:26, Deuteronomy 28:58-62

C. Sickness is from Devil, and not God—Job, Acts 10:38, Hebrews 2:14-15, I John 3:8

D. Deliverance from sickness is provided for in the Atonement and is the privilege for all believers—Isaiah 53:4-5, Matthew 8:16-17, I Peter 2:24

    a. Jesus came to minister to the entire person, body, soul, and spirit

    b. Forgiveness and healing are blessings from God to make us whole

E. Healing is an integral part of the Gospel—Luke 4:18-19, Luke 10:9, Matthew 10:7, Mark 16:15-20

F. Jesus himself commanded it—Mark 16: 17-18

G. We are to practice healing as a part of our Christian walk—James 5:14-16

    a. Call the elders—accountability

    b. Pray for the one who is sick action

    c. Anoint with oil—symbolizes the work of the Holy Spirit

    d. Faith—trusting God to do the work

H. Just as Jesus did not have a set formula, we must not get into a "healing ritual" but rather trust God to heal us. He often will use the miraculous, and will also use others (doctors and medicine)

I. Purpose of healing—to bring Glory to God

J.   Why are not everyone healed?

    a.   We are still in human bodies that get old and sick

    b.   Sometimes people "enjoy" being sick

    c.   The principal of "reaping what you sow"

    d.   God may be glorified more by a person's infirmity

    e.   There will be the "Ultimate Healing"—new bodies that will not have sickness or pain

SUPPLEMENTAL MATERIAL

Bible Reading Plan
Surrender List
A Declaration

BIBLE READING PLAN

Galatians 4:19

John—Jesus is God

Matthew—Jesus is King

Luke—Jesus is Man

Mark—Jesus is Servant

Acts—Jesus is in the Church

Hebrews—Jesus fulfills the Old Testament

Revelation—Jesus in Future

Romans, James—Personal Conduct

I & II Corinthians, Galatians, Philippians, Ephesians, Colossians, I & II Thessalonians—Letters of Conduct within the Church

I & II Timothy, Titus, Philemon—Personal letters regarding Leadership

I & II Peter, I, II & III John, Jude—Warning against False Teachers

SURRENDER LIST

Name: _____

"Let us lay aside every weight" Hebrews 12:1

Spouse: _____

Former Spouse (if any): _____

Children: _____

_____

Grandchildren (if any): _____

_____

Parents/In-laws (if living): _____

_____

Grandparents (if living): _____

_____

Home: _____

Other Property: _____

Automobile(s): _____

Other Vehicles (boats/RV/motorcycles,etc.): _____

_____

_____

Pets/Animals: _____

_____

Hobbies/Sports:_____

_____

Business/Job:_____

_____

Favorite Possession: _____

_____

Most Valuable Possession: _____

_____

Investments/Plans for Future: _____

_____

_____

Household Items: _____

_____

_____

_____

_____

_____

Electronics (Computers/TV, etc.): _____

_____

_____

Entertainment (Movies/Videos/Games/Music, etc.)

_____

_____

_____

_____

_____

Art Work/Photos: _____

_____

_____

Supplemental Material

Family Heirlooms/Inherited Items:_____

_____

_____

Military Service: _____

_____

Boss/Co-workers: _____

_____

_____

Friends: _____

_____

Other Family (Brothers/Sisters etc.) _____

_____

_____

_____

_____

Toys: _____

_____

Money: _____

Dreams: _____

_____

_____

Fears:_____

_____

_____

Feelings: _____

_____

_____

Emotions: _____

_____

_____

Addictions: _____

_____

_____

Ministries/Gifts: _____

_____

_____

Other: _____

_____

_____

A DECLARATION

I, _____, having accepted Jesus as my savior

And being cleaned from all sin by the Blood of Jesus

Do hereby declare that I have been anointed with oil

According to Leviticus 8:12 & 23 to be a Priest in accordance

With 1st Peter 2:9 & 10 to be a Royal Priesthood,

A Holy Nation, a Chosen Generation and a

Peculiar Person, set apart for the purpose of giving

Praise unto my Lord, Savior, King, Brother,

And Friend, Jesus Christ.

I am hereby given the rank of Knight of the Cross of Christ

For the purpose of serving Jesus Christ

In any way that He would ask.

Dated this _____ date of _____ , 20____

Signed: _____